THE ULTIMATE VOLLEYBALL COACHING GUIDE

Essential Drills, Volleyball Fundamentals, Skill Progressions, and Mental Toughness Tools

---

RILEY RUSH

Copyright © 2026 Riley Rush

All rights reserved. No part of this publication may be reproduced, distributed, or transmitted in any form or by any means, including photocopying, recording, or other electronic or mechanical methods, without the prior written permission of the publisher, except in the case of brief quotations embodied in critical reviews and certain other noncommercial uses permitted by copyright law.

Trademarked names appear throughout this book. Rather than using a trademark symbol with every occurrence of a trademarked name, names are used in an editorial fashion, with no intention of infringing on the respective owner's trademark. The information in this book is distributed on an as-is basis, without warranty. Although every precaution has been taken in the preparation of this work, neither the author nor the publisher shall have any liability to any person or entity, with respect to any loss or damage caused, or alleged to be caused, directly or indirectly, by the information contained in this book.

A good coach can change a game. A great coach can change a life.

— *John Wooden*

Contents

Introduction — vi

Part I
Stepping Into Coaching

1. Welcome to Your First Season — 3
2. Understanding Your Role — 7
3. Coaching Mindset for the Whole Season — 14

Part II
Pre-Season Foundations

4. Setting Up Your Season Blueprint — 23
5. Team Tryouts & Player Assessments — 28
6. Creating Your Team Culture — 32
7. Teaching the Basics: Essential Skills to Master Early — 36
8. Building Mental Toughness: The Four Pillars — 41
9. Your First Practices: Structure, Warmups, and Early Teaching Cues — 44

Part III
Managing the Season

10. Your First Games: What to Expect — 51
11. Tournament Survival Guide — 55
12. Mid-Season Reflection & Adjustments — 58
13. Burnout Prevention & Emotional Support — 61

Part IV
Advanced Coaching Flow

14. Running Competitive, High-Energy Practices — 67
15. Troubleshooting Common Problems — 70
16. Parent Communication Mastery — 73

Part V
End-of-Season Excellence

17. Preparing for Finals & Big Events — 79
18. End-of-Year Success: What Really Matters — 82
19. Looking Ahead to Year Two — 87

Part VI
The 25 Core Drills Every Coach Needs

Structured Play Development	93
Drill 1: Serving with a Purpose	97
Drill 2: Passing with Consistency	101
Drill 3: Setting for Accuracy	105
Drill 4: No-Net Pepper	108
Drill 5: Communication Triangle Drill	111
Drill 6: Serving Under Pressure	114
Drill 7: Block Jump Timing	117
Drill 8: Coverage Chaos	120
Drill 9: First Ball Side-Out	123
Drill 10: Serve-Receive Circuits	126
Drill 11: Transition Attack	129
Drill 12: Defensive Read & Reaction	132
Drill 13: Dig & Cover Circuit	136
Drill 14: Setter Decision Challenge	139
Drill 15: Attack Coverage & Continuation	142
Drill 16: Team Serve-Receive Rotation	145
Drill 17: Quick Offense Coordination	148
Drill 18: Serve & Transition Defense	151
Drill 19: Game Simulation: Controlled Rally	154
Drill 20: Pressure Game Scenarios	157
Drill 21: Advanced Read-Based Blocking	160
Drill 22: Extended Rally Defensive Control	163
Drill 23: Situational Serving Strategy	166
Drill 24: Competitive Team Challenge	169
Drill 25: Full-Court Chaos Game	172
Conclusion	175
References	177

Introduction

Coaching volleyball is about more than teaching athletes how to pass, serve, or spike. It's about guiding young players through challenges, helping them discover confidence, and creating an environment where growth and joy go hand in hand. For new coaches, the role can feel overwhelming—balancing drills, communication, and expectations from players and parents. For experienced coaches, the challenge often lies in staying organized, keeping practices fresh, and maintaining energy across a long season. This book is designed to meet both needs: to give you practical tools, clear strategies, and a philosophy that keeps players at the center of everything you do.

Inside, you'll find simple, actionable steps for building strong fundamentals, designing practices that flow, and creating a team culture that players love. You'll learn how to manage energy and emotions, how to support athletes through setbacks, and how to keep yourself grounded as a coach. Alongside skill progressions and essential drills, you'll discover ways to foster mental toughness, resilience, and confidence—qualities that matter just as much off the court as they do during a match.

This guide is not about theory for theory's sake. It's about giving you the essentials you can use right away: how to structure your season, how to keep practices engaging, how to handle tough moments with calmness, and how to celebrate growth at every stage.

At its core, this book is built on one philosophy: players come first. When you coach with clarity, empathy, and purpose, you don't just build better athletes—you build stronger people. And that is the true measure of coaching success.

As you step into this journey, remember: every drill, every practice, and every conversation is an opportunity to shape lives. This book is here to help you make the most of those moments.

PART I
Stepping Into Coaching

ONE

Welcome to Your First Season

So, you're a coach. Maybe you said yes because your daughter's team needed someone, maybe you're a former player who misses the game, or maybe you just have a heart for helping young athletes grow. Whatever the reason, you're here. Welcome. Take a deep breath, because you are in for one of the most challenging, chaotic, and deeply rewarding experiences of your life.

Before we dive into drills, rotations, and practice plans, we need to start with the one thing that will anchor you through every tough loss, every messy practice, and every moment of self-doubt: your coaching philosophy. This isn't some dusty academic thesis; it's your internal compass. It's the simple, core belief system that guides your decisions when things get loud and confusing. It's what helps you know what to do and, more importantly, why you're doing it.

The Player-First Compass: Your True North

If there is one guiding principle that should shape every decision you make this season, it is this: put the player first. This philosophy is simple in theory but requires constant, conscious effort in practice. It means that every drill you run, every piece of feedback you give, and every system you implement should be designed to serve the long-term growth and well-being of your athletes.

A player-first approach is built on three core pillars that act as your "True North," always pointing you in the right direction.

Pillar	Description
Connection	Before you can coach a player, you have to connect with them. Learn their names, ask about their day, and show them that you care about them as people. A strong connection builds the trust necessary for effective coaching.
Confidence	Your primary job is to be a confidence builder. Young athletes are often their own harshest critics. Your voice needs to be the one that reminds them of their potential, celebrates their progress, and encourages them to keep going when they want to give up.
Growth	Focus on the process, not the outcome. Are your players getting better? Are they learning to be good teammates? Are they developing a love for the game? If the answer is yes, then you are succeeding, regardless of what the scoreboard says.

Building Your Coaching GPS: The "How"

Your philosophy is your compass, but you still need a map to navigate the season. Think of it as your coaching GPS—a system that helps you make smart, consistent decisions. Here's how to build it, step-by-step.

Step 1: Find Your "Why" (Your Destination)

Before you can plan a route, you need to know where you're going. Why are you coaching? What is the ultimate goal for your season? This isn't about winning a championship; it's about the impact you want to have. Your "why" is the destination you're always driving toward.

Maybe your "why" is:

- To be the coach I wish I'd had.
- To create a space where young boys/girls can feel strong, confident, and supported.
- To teach young athletes that hard work can be joyful.

Your "why" is your anchor. When a game gets stressful or a practice goes off the rails, remembering your core purpose will keep you grounded.

Step 2: Choose Your "Roads" (Your Principles)

Your principles are the roads you take to reach your destination. They are the guiding beliefs that inform your actions. Many new coaches choose their principles in a few common ways:

- The Rearview Mirror Method: Coaching exactly how you were coached. This can be a great starting point, but it can also mean repeating outdated or ineffective methods (like punishing mistakes with running) just because they're familiar.
- The Blueprint Method: Copying the practice plan of a highly successful college or club team. While it's smart to learn from the best, what works for elite 18-year-olds may not work for your 12-year-old team.
- The Inventor's Workshop Method: Making it all up as you go. Creativity is fantastic, but without a foundation in proven methods, your coaching can become inconsistent and confusing for your players.

The most effective approach is the Explorer's Method. An explorer learns from maps (research), observes the landscape (watches other great coaches), and then adapts based on the terrain in front of them (what their specific team needs). This book is your map, but you are the explorer.

Step 3: Set Your "Guardrails" (Your Values)

Values are the guardrails on your road. They keep you from veering off course, especially when emotions are running high. They are your non-negotiables. What behaviors will you model and expect from your team, no matter what?

Your values might include:

- Integrity: We do the right thing, even when it's hard.
- Resilience: We get back up after we fall, and we help our teammates up, too.
- Joy: We work hard, but we also remember to have fun and celebrate our successes.

When a referee makes a bad call, your values will determine whether you react with anger or with calm leadership. When a player is struggling, your values will guide you to respond with patience and support. Your players will forget the drills you ran, but they will remember the values you lived by.

Making It Stick: Your Coaching Toolkit

A philosophy is only useful if you can remember it in the moment. Here are two simple tools to keep your philosophy front and center.

1. The Three-Word Mantra: Condense your entire philosophy into a short, memorable phrase. Write it on your clipboard, your water bottle, or the top of your practice plan. It's your quick-glance reminder of what matters.

Examples:

- "Compete with Joy."
- "Effort is Everything."
- "Lift Each Other."

2. The Filter Question: When you have to make a tough decision, ask yourself one simple question that filters it through your philosophy.

Examples:

- "Will this build or break trust with my players?"
- "Does this help my team grow as people?"
- "Is this decision rooted in patience and respect?"

The Journey Ahead

Stepping into your first season can feel like standing at the base of a mountain. There will be steep climbs, unexpected storms, and moments where you question if you have what it takes. But there will also be breathtaking views, moments of pure joy, and the profound satisfaction of knowing you are making a difference.

You don't have to be a perfect coach. You just have to be a coach who leads with intention. By building your philosophy from the ground up, you've already taken the most important step. Let's get started.

TWO

Understanding Your Role

Now that you've built your coaching philosophy and understand why you're stepping into this role, it's time to get practical. What does your job actually look like? What are your responsibilities? What boundaries do you need to set? And how do you build the trust that makes everything else possible?

This chapter is about clarity. When you deeply understand your role, you show up with confidence. Your players sense that. Your players' parents sense that. And suddenly, everything gets easier.

The Foundation: What Your Role Actually Is

Your job has layers. You are not just a drill instructor or a strategist. You are a leader, a teacher, and someone who shapes how young athletes see themselves. Let's break down what that means in practice.

You Set the Tone

Everything your team does, thinks, and feels starts with you. Your energy in the gym is contagious. If you walk in calm and focused, your team will be calm and focused, too. If you walk in stressed and scattered, they will mirror that too. Your mood isn't just your mood—it's the emotional climate of your entire team.

This doesn't mean you have to be happy all the time. It means you show up intentionally. You manage your own stress so you can be present for theirs. You handle mistakes with patience. You respond to pressure with steadiness. Your players are always watching how you handle adversity, and that's what they'll learn to do.

You Make the Decisions

As the coach, you have the authority to make decisions about practice structure, lineups, playing time, and team standards. These decisions should come from your philosophy and your principles, not from emotion or pressure. When you make a decision, own it. Explain it if needed, but don't apologize for it or second-guess it in front of your team. Consistency builds trust.

You Communicate

Communication is your most powerful tool. You communicate with your players about skills, strategy, and expectations. You communicate with parents about progress, challenges, and ways they can support their child. You communicate with your director or athletic director about needs and concerns. Clear, honest communication prevents most problems before they start.

You Support Growth

Your core job is to help each athlete improve—not just as a volleyball player, but as a person. This means you notice effort, celebrate progress, and respond to setbacks with encouragement. You create an environment where mistakes are part of learning, not something to fear.

Building Trust: The Currency of Coaching

Everything else in this chapter leads to one thing: trust. When your players trust you, they will run through walls for you. When their parents trust you, they will support you, even when they don't agree with every decision. Trust is the foundation of everything.

Trust isn't built in one big moment; it's built in small moments, over and over again. Here's how:

Show Up Consistently

Be the same person every day. Be the same person in practice and in games. Be the same person with your best player and your last player on the bench. Consistency teaches people they can count on you. When players know what to expect, they relax. When they relax, they learn faster and perform better.

Care About Them as People

Ask about their day. Remember what they're working on. Notice when they look off and check in. Celebrate their small improvements. When a player knows you care about them as a person—not just as a volleyball player—they will go so much further as an athlete. Trust is the soil where everything else grows.

Live Your Values

Your values aren't just words on a whiteboard. They show up in how you treat people, how you handle mistakes, and how you react to pressure. If you say you value respect but you yell at referees, your team will notice. If you say you value effort but you only praise winning, your team will notice. Your actions are your loudest teaching tool.

Be Honest

Tell the truth, even when it's uncomfortable. If a player isn't getting playing time because they need to improve a specific skill, tell them that. If you made a mistake in a decision, own it. Honesty builds respect. It shows your players that you see them clearly and that you're not afraid to have real conversations.

Managing Expectations: Yours and Theirs

One of the biggest sources of conflict in coaching comes from misaligned expectations. You expect one thing, parents expect another, and players expect something completely different. Before the season starts, get clear on what everyone is expecting.

Your Expectations

First, get clear on what you expect. What does a successful season look like? What standards will you hold your team to? What does effort look like? What does respect look like? What does improvement look like? Write these down. Be specific. "I expect effort" is too vague. "I expect players to communicate on every play, move their feet to the ball, and stay positive even after mistakes" is clear.

Player Expectations

Your players need to know what you expect from them. This should be communicated clearly, multiple times, and in writing. Cover:

- What they should bring to practice (water, attitude, focus).
- What happens if they're late or miss practice.
- How playing time is earned.
- What good sportsmanship looks like.
- How they should treat each other and the other team.

Parent Expectations

Parents need to know what to expect from you and what you expect from them. This is best done in a pre-season meeting or in a written document. Cover:

- Your coaching philosophy and what it means.
- How communication will work (when and how you'll contact them, when they can contact you).
- How playing time decisions are made.
- What they can do to support their child's development.
- What topics are open for discussion and what topics are not (for example, playing time of other players is off-limits).

Setting Boundaries: The Key to Your Survival

As a new coach, your instinct will be to give everything to your team. That's a beautiful impulse, but it's also the fastest path to burnout. Healthy boundaries aren't selfish; they are essential for your well-being and your effectiveness as a coach.

Time Boundaries

You do not need to be available 24/7. Set specific times when you will respond to emails or texts. It's okay to let a non-urgent message wait until the next day. If you're coaching in the evening, you don't need to be answering parent emails at midnight. Set a cutoff time and stick to it.

Emotional Boundaries

You can be empathetic to a player's or parent's frustration without taking it on as your own. Listen, support, and then let it go. Their emotions are not your responsibility to carry. If a parent is upset about playing time, you can listen to their perspective without absorbing their anger. You can be kind and firm at the same time.

Role Boundaries

You are the coach, not the parent, the therapist, or the academic advisor. Know where your role begins and ends. If a player is struggling with something outside of volleyball—family issues, school stress, mental health concerns—you can be supportive and caring, but you should also point them toward resources that are better equipped to help. You can say, "I notice you seem stressed. Have you talked to the school counselor?" You don't have to be the one to solve it.

The 24-Hour Rule

This is one of the most valuable boundaries you can set with parents. If a parent has an issue or concern—especially about playing time—they must wait 24 hours after a game or tournament to contact you. This allows emotions to cool and leads to a much more productive conversation. Implement this rule from day one, and communicate it clearly. Most parents will respect it. The ones who don't will teach you something about their expectations.

Communication with Parents: The System That Works

Clear, proactive communication with parents prevents most problems before they start. Here's a system that works:

The Pre-Season Meeting

Before the first practice, hold a meeting for all parents. This is your chance to introduce yourself, share your coaching philosophy, and set expectations for the season. Cover:

- Your coaching background and why you're coaching.
- Your philosophy and what it means in practice.
- Practice schedule and any expectations around attendance.
- How you'll communicate with them and how they can communicate with you.
- How playing time decisions are made.
- What you expect from parents in terms of support and behavior.

This meeting sets the tone for the entire season. Parents who feel informed and included from the beginning are much less likely to become frustrated later.

Define What's Open for Discussion

Be clear about what you are happy to discuss and what you are not.

- Open for discussion: Your child's development, what they can work on, how they can be a better teammate, their attitude or effort, what's happening in practice.
- Not open for discussion: Playing time of other players, team strategy, other players' behavior or skills, decisions about who starts or who sits.

This protects your team's unity and prevents you from being put in awkward positions.

Proactive Updates

Don't wait for parents to ask questions. Send regular updates about what the team is working on, what's going well, and what players can work on at home. This keeps parents feeling connected and informed. It also prevents them from imagining worst-case scenarios when they don't hear from you.

The Role of Your Director or Athletic Director

If you're coaching at a club or school, you have someone above you—a director, athletic director, or program coordinator. This person is your ally, not your adversary. Get to know them early.

WHAT TO DISCUSS

Before your first practice, meet with this person and talk about:

- What the season is expected to look like.
- How communication will work between you and them.
- Any important rules or guidelines you need to follow.
- How they can support you when tough situations come up.
- What resources are available to you.

WHY THIS MATTERS

When parents have questions or concerns, this is the person who has your back. When you need guidance on a difficult situation, this is who you call. Building a strong relationship with your director early makes the whole season easier.

Your Role as a Model

Remember this: your players are always watching. Not just how you coach, but how you live. How you handle a bad call from a referee. How you treat the opposing team. How you respond when things don't go your way. How you talk about yourself and others. You are teaching lessons far bigger than volleyball. You are teaching your players what it looks like to be a good person. Make sure you're modeling the values you want them to have.

The Bottom Line

Your role is to be a steady, caring, clear leader. You don't have to be perfect. You just have to be consistent, honest, and genuinely invested in your players' growth. When you do that, everything else falls into place.

THREE

Coaching Mindset for the Whole Season

We spend so much time thinking about our players' mindsets that we often forget about the most important one in the gym: our own. Your inner state—your confidence, your calmness, your emotional regulation, and your energy—is the invisible force that shapes everything. It dictates how you teach, how you lead, and how your players feel the moment they walk into practice.

This chapter is about managing your own inner game. Because when you are grounded, confident, and calm, you create the space for your players to become the same.

The Coach's Growth Mindset: Your Foundation for Confidence

Mindset is the quiet engine behind every athlete's growth. It shapes how players respond to challenges, how they handle mistakes, and how they show up for each other. Research shows that people tend to operate from one of two core belief systems:

- Fixed Mindset: The belief that abilities are set in stone. You're either a natural setter or you're not. Either you have the vertical jump or you don't.
- Growth Mindset: The belief that abilities can be developed through deliberate practice, quality coaching, and persistence.

No one is 100% one or the other; we all slide back and forth depending on the situation. The goal isn't perfection; it's awareness and intentional shifts. And here's the best part: mindsets are not permanent. With the right environment and intentional coaching, a fixed belief can become flexible. This transformation starts with you.

Two Powerful Analogies to Teach Your Players (and Yourself)

To make this concept stick, use concrete stories your players can visualize. Here are two original analogies that work powerfully in the gym.

1. BUILDING MUSCLE MEMORY LIKE BUILDING A HOUSE

Think of a new skill like building a house. On the first day, the foundation is rough and uneven. The walls go up slowly, and everything feels fragile. A player learning to pass might feel like they're building on shaky ground—every mistake feels like the whole structure might collapse.

But here's what actually happens: with each rep, the foundation gets stronger. The walls get straighter. The roof gets more secure. After weeks of consistent work, that house is solid. It can withstand storms. It's reliable. And the player who built it didn't become a different person; they just kept showing up and adding one brick at a time.

The key insight? The house wasn't built in a day, and neither is a volleyball skill. Progress isn't always visible week to week, but it's happening. Every practice is another brick.

2. THE SKILL SPIRAL: GOING DEEPER, NOT JUST WIDER

Imagine a spiral staircase. When you first learn to pass, you're on the bottom step. You're learning the basic platform, the footwork, the contact point. That's step one.

But as you practice, you don't just repeat the same step over and over. You go up. Now you're learning to pass different types of serves. You're learning to move your feet faster. You're learning to read the server's motion. That's step two.

Keep spiraling up. Now you're passing in game situations. You're communicating with your setter. You're adjusting on the fly. That's step three.

The beautiful part? You're still doing the same basic skill—passing—but you're doing it at a deeper level. This is what growth looks like. It's not about learning 100 new things; it's about mastering one thing at increasingly complex levels.

How Your Words Shape Their Mindset

Your words have the power to build or break a growth mindset culture. The rule is simple: praise the action, not the identity.

- Identity Praise (Fixed): "You're such a great defender!" This sounds nice, but it tells the player their success comes from an innate gift. Now, when they struggle, it feels like a personal failure.

- Action Praise (Growth): "The way you read that hitter's shoulder and adjusted your positioning—that's exactly what I'm talking about." This tells the player their success came from a specific, repeatable action. Now, they know how to do it again.

The difference sounds small, but it changes everything. Players praised for their actions seek out challenges because they know challenges are how they improve. Players praised for their identity avoid challenges because they're afraid of damaging their image.

Teach your players to praise each other this way, too. When they learn to say, "I loved how you stayed low and kept moving your feet on that dig," instead of just "Nice dig," you multiply the amount of growth-minded feedback in your gym. Peer feedback is powerful—almost half of what your players learn comes from each other, not from you.

Coaches Need a Growth Mindset, Too

It's easy to demand a growth mindset from our players while we stay firmly planted in our own fixed-mindset comfort zone. Coaches fall into traps constantly:

- The "Proven Method" Trap: Sticking to the same drills and systems because they've worked before, even if they're not working now.
- The "I Should Know This" Trap: Avoiding asking for help or feedback because you're afraid of looking unprepared.
- The "My Way" Trap: Believing your approach is the only right approach, and dismissing new ideas or different perspectives.

Here's the truth: coaches without a growth mindset plateau just as fast as athletes. Your players learn more from how you handle your own mistakes than from anything else. When you try a new drill and it flops, do you get defensive, or do you say, "That didn't work the way I planned. Let's adjust"? When you admit you're still learning, you give your players permission to be learners too.

Understanding Mindset on the Court: How It Shows Up in Real Situations

Mindset isn't just a theory. It shows up in real moments, every single practice. Here's how to recognize it:

Situation	Fixed Mindset Response	Growth Mindset Response
After a tough loss	"We're just not good enough." "Other teams are better."	"What did we learn? What can we adjust?"
When a drill is hard	"This is too hard. I'm not getting it."	"This is challenging. That means I'm learning something new."
When receiving feedback	"She's criticizing me." "I'm doing it wrong."	"This is useful information. How can I apply it?"
When a teammate succeeds	"I wish I could do that." "That's not fair."	"Look what's possible. I can work toward that, too."
When making a mistake	"I always mess this up." "I'm not cut out for this."	"What went wrong? How do I fix it next time?"

Your job isn't to eliminate fixed responses—they're human. Your job is to coach athletes toward more productive ones. When you see a fixed response, gently redirect. "I hear your frustration. That's a tough situation. What's one thing you can control right now?"

A Real Coaching Moment: When Adversity Becomes a Teacher

Picture this: Your team is in a tournament on a brutally humid day. The gym is sweltering. You can see frustration rising—the classic fixed mindset signs. Players are complaining about the heat. They're comparing themselves to the other team ("They look so fresh"). They're making excuses ("It's too hot to focus").

Instead of lecturing about mindset, you ask a simple question: "What's one thing we can control right now?"

Suddenly, the conversation shifts. "We can hydrate between matches." "We can take breaks in the hallway." "We can focus on our side of the court, not theirs." "We can adjust our pace to conserve energy."

The heat didn't change. The gym didn't get cooler. But their mindset did. And when they won that tournament, it wasn't because the conditions improved—it was because they learned to problem-solve instead of complain.

The Internal Traffic Light: Your Tool for Emotional Regulation

Your emotional state is the thermostat for the entire gym. The key is to recognize your own emotional state before it starts to affect your players. The easiest way to do this is with the "Internal Traffic Light."

- Green Light: You are calm, present, and focused. You are seeing the game clearly. Your feedback is constructive. You are in control.
- Yellow Light: You are starting to feel stressed, rushed, or frustrated. Your heart rate is up. You're second-guessing your decisions. Your feedback is getting sharper. You are starting to lose control.
- Red Light: You are overwhelmed, angry, or completely checked out. You are reacting emotionally instead of responding thoughtfully. You are not coaching anymore; you are just surviving.

Your job is not to stay in the green light all the time—that's impossible. Your job is to recognize when you're in the yellow and have a strategy to get back to green before you hit red.

Your "Back to Green" Strategies:

- The Anchor Breath: Take one slow, deliberate breath. Inhale for four seconds, hold for four, exhale for four. This simple action resets your nervous system.
- The Sideline Step-Back: Physically take two steps back from the court. This small movement creates mental distance and gives you a moment to reset your perspective.
- The Mantra Moment: Silently repeat your three-word philosophy from Chapter 1. "Compete with Joy." "Effort is Everything." This reminds you of what truly matters.

Sustainable Energy: How to Survive the Season Without Burning Out

Coaching is a marathon, not a sprint. Your passion and energy are your greatest assets, but they are also finite resources. If you give everything you have in the first month, you will have nothing left for the championship push. Here's how to manage your energy so you can finish the season as strong as you started.

Energy Management Strategy	How to Implement It
The "Good Enough" Practice Plan	Your practice plan does not need to be a work of art. It needs to be clear, focused, and effective. Don't spend three hours crafting the "perfect" plan. Spend 30 minutes creating a "good enough" plan that hits your key objectives. Done is better than perfect.
The "Off" Switch	When you are not coaching, don't coach. Don't spend your entire evening replaying the game in your head. Don't let parent emails interrupt your family dinner. Set a time each night when you put coaching away. Your brain needs to rest and recharge.
The Energy Givers and Takers	Make a list of the things that give you energy and the things that drain your energy. Energy givers might be listening to a podcast on your way to practice, spending five minutes chatting with your assistant coach, or watching your team finally nail a new skill. Energy takers might be dealing with a difficult parent, worrying about playing time, or spending too much time on administrative tasks. Do more of what gives you energy and find ways to minimize or streamline what drains you.
The "One Thing" Focus	You cannot fix everything at once. At the beginning of each practice, choose one thing you want your team to get better at that day. Just one. This simplifies your focus, makes your feedback more effective, and prevents you from feeling overwhelmed by all the things that need work.

The Heart of the Matter

Your mindset is the source code for your coaching. It determines how you show up, how you lead, and how you make your players feel. You don't have to be a perfect, unflappable guru. You just have to be a coach who is self-aware, intentional, and willing to grow right alongside your team. When you master your own inner game, you give your players the greatest gift of all: a leader who is steady, confident, and ready for whatever the season brings.

PART II
Pre-Season Foundations

FOUR

Setting Up Your Season Blueprint

Welcome to the architect phase of your coaching season. Before you can build a strong team, you need a blueprint. This isn't about scripting every single practice from day one; it's about creating a clear, simple guide that will keep you focused, organized, and intentional all season long. A good blueprint prevents you from getting lost in the weeds of weekly drills and helps you build something that lasts.

This chapter will walk you through the three essential parts of your season blueprint: defining what success really looks like, understanding the unique needs of your age group, and creating a simple, three-phase plan for the entire season.

Step 1: Define Your "North Star" (What Success Looks Like)

Before you plan a single drill, you need to define your destination. What is the ultimate goal of this season? Here's a hint: it's probably not winning a championship. For youth athletes, the scoreboard is the least important measure of a successful season.

Your "North Star" is your one, core objective—the guiding principle that will anchor every decision you make. It's the thing you'll come back to after a tough loss or a frustrating practice. It's the reason you said yes to coaching in the first place.

Choose one of these as your primary objective, or write your own. Keep it somewhere you can see it every day.

North Star Objective	What It Looks Like in Practice
Ignite a Lifelong Love for the Game	Your practices are fun, engaging, and full of positive energy. Players are excited to come to the gym and sad when practice is over.
Cultivate Unshakeable Confidence	You create a safe environment where mistakes are treated as learning opportunities. You praise effort and progress, and every player leaves the season feeling more capable than when they started.
Master the Fundamentals	You are relentlessly focused on teaching skills the right way. Your drills are clear, your feedback is precise, and your players develop a strong technical foundation that will serve them for years.
Forge Resilient Teammates	You teach your players how to communicate, how to support each other, and how to handle adversity with grace. They learn that being a good teammate is just as important as being a good player.

Your North Star is your filter. When you're deciding between two drills, ask yourself: "Which one gets us closer to our North Star?" When you're dealing with a conflict, ask: "What response aligns with our North Star?" These simple questions will bring clarity to almost any coaching dilemma.

Step 2: Know Your Age Group (Your Roadmap)

Once you know your destination, you need a roadmap that's appropriate for your travelers. Coaching 12-year-olds is fundamentally different from coaching 17-year-olds. Their physical abilities, emotional maturity, and what they need from a coach are worlds apart. Understanding these differences is key to creating a successful season.

Here is a simple guide to the different stages of a youth volleyball player's journey.

Age Group	The Coaching Focus (Your Role)
12 & Under (The "Spark" Age)	Your primary job is to make it fun. These athletes are brand new to the sport, and your goal is to ignite a spark. Focus on fundamentals taught through games, not rigid drills. Celebrate small victories, like a good toss or a three-touch rally. Success is watching a player's face light up when a skill finally "clicks."
14 & Under (The "Bridge" Age)	Most of these players have some experience, but they're still connecting the dots. Your role is to be a bridge between basic skills and real gameplay. You can start introducing simple systems (like a 4-2), defined positions, and more structured drills. They are ready for more but still need patience and positive reinforcement.
16 & Under (The "Commitment" Age)	This is where things get more serious. Many of these athletes are trying to make their high school teams or are committed to playing competitively. Your practices should be more structured, your feedback more detailed, and your expectations higher. They are ready for more complex strategies and a faster pace of play.
18 & Under (The "Performance" Age)	These are experienced athletes who are here to compete. Some are hoping for college opportunities. Your role is to refine their skills, manage complex team systems, and prepare them to perform under pressure. You are less of a skill teacher and more of a strategic manager and mental coach.

Tailor your expectations, your communication style, and your practice plans to the age group you're coaching. What works for a 16s team will overwhelm a 12s team, and what works for a 12s team will bore a 16s team.

Step 3: Build Your Three-Phase Season Plan (The Blueprint)

A season can feel long and overwhelming without a plan. Instead of thinking about it as one long stretch, break it down into three simple phases. This gives your season a natural rhythm and ensures you're focusing on the right things at the right time.

PHASE 1: THE FOUNDATION (FIRST 1-3 WEEKS)

- The Goal: Build your team culture and establish a strong fundamental base.
- What to Focus On:
- Culture: Set your team standards, teach your communication cues, and get to know your players as people.

- Fundamentals: Dedicate the vast majority of your practice time to high-rep, fundamental drills. Passing, serving, setting, and basic footwork are the priorities.
- Simple Systems: Introduce your base offense and defense in its simplest form.
- The Vibe: Low pressure, high energy, and lots of positive reinforcement.

Phase 2: The Integration (The Middle of the Season)

- The Goal: Start combining skills and applying them in more game-like situations.
- What to Focus On:
- Combining Skills: Move from isolated drills (e.g., just passing) to drills that combine skills (e.g., serve, pass, set, hit). (The last section of the book provides drills that merge skills into full game cycles.)
- Game-Like Situations: Use drills that force players to read and react. Small-sided games (3v3, 4v4) are perfect for this phase.
- Team Chemistry: Focus on how your players work together. Who communicates well? Who struggles under pressure? This is where you learn the personality of your team.
- The Vibe: More competitive, more challenging, and focused on problem-solving.

Phase 3: The Performance (Last 1-3 Weeks Before Championships)

- The Goal: Sharpen your team's execution and prepare them to compete at their best.
- What to Focus On:
- Competitive Drills: Run drills that have a winner and a loser. Put something on the line (even if it's just bragging rights). This simulates the pressure of a real game.
- Scrimmaging (playing a practice match that simulates real-game situations): Spend a significant portion of practice scrimmaging, either against another team or inter-squad. This is where you fine-tune your lineups and strategies.
- Mental Toughness: Talk explicitly about how to handle pressure, how to bounce back from mistakes, and how to stay focused in big moments.
- The Vibe: Focused, intense, and confident.

Your Blueprint in Action

Your season blueprint is not a rigid script; it's a guide. It gives you direction and purpose. When you combine your "North Star" objective, your understanding of your age group, and your three-phase plan, you have a powerful tool that will keep you and your team on track all season long.

You know where you're going. You know the right roadmap for your team. And you have a simple, phase-by-phase plan to get there. You're not just a coach anymore. You're an architect. Now, let's go build something great.

FIVE

Team Tryouts & Player Assessments

Tryouts can be one of the most stressful parts of the season—for players, for parents, and especially for you. It's a high-stakes environment where dreams can feel like they're on the line. But it doesn't have to be that way. With a clear plan and a positive approach, you can turn tryouts from a stressful ordeal into an exciting, organized, and encouraging experience for everyone involved.

This chapter is your guide to running a smooth, effective, and positive tryout. We'll cover what to look for beyond just skill, how to evaluate players fairly, and a step-by-step flow that will make your tryout feel less like a judgment day and more like the first day of a great season.

What to Look For: The Three Pillars of a Great Teammate

It's easy to get mesmerized by the player with the hardest hit or the highest jump. But the best players aren't always the most skilled; they're the ones who make the whole team better. When you're evaluating talent, look for three things:

1. Skill (The "What"): This is the most obvious one. Can they pass, set, hit, and serve? Do they have a solid technical foundation? This is the baseline. But don't just look at their best rep; look at their average. Consistency is more valuable than occasional brilliance.
2. Athleticism (The "How"): How do they move? Are they quick, agile, and coordinated? Do they have good body control? A player who is a great athlete but has raw skills can often develop faster than a skilled player who is not athletic. You can teach technique, but you can't teach speed.
3. Intangibles (The "Who"): This is the most important and most overlooked pillar. This is about character. What kind of teammate will this player be? How do they respond to a mistake? Do they make eye contact when you're talking? Do they cheer for others? A player with a great attitude and a willingness to learn is worth their weight in gold.

Rule of Thumb: When in doubt, choose the player with the better attitude. Skill can be taught. Character is much harder to coach.

How to Evaluate: A Simple and Fair System

To run a fair tryout, you need a simple, consistent way to evaluate every player. Don't try to keep it all in your head. Use a clipboard and a simple rating scale. For each key skill, rate players on a 1-3 scale.

- 1 = Needs Significant Work: The player is still in the very early stages of learning this skill.
- 2 = Developing/Inconsistent: The player shows flashes of good technique but is inconsistent.
- 3 = Solid/Consistent: The player has a strong technical foundation and can execute the skill consistently.

You should also have a section for notes on athleticism and intangibles. Did they hustle for every ball? Did they listen intently during instructions? Did they encourage a teammate? Write it down.

Here is a sample evaluation sheet you can adapt:

Player Number	Passing (1-3)	Serving (1-3)	Hitting (1-3)	Setting (1-3)	Athleticism Notes	Intangibles Notes
#12	2	3	2	1	Quick feet, good first step	Made eye contact, asked a good question
#15	3	2	3	1	High vertical, powerful	Cheered for others, hustled

Positive Tryout Flow: A Step-by-Step Guide

A great tryout is organized, efficient, and makes every player feel seen and valued, regardless of whether they make the team. Here is a simple, step-by-step flow that works for any age group.

Step 1: The Welcome (5 Minutes)

Start on time. Gather all the players in a circle. Welcome them, thank them for being there, and tell them how excited you are. Briefly explain what the tryout will look like. Your calm, positive energy will set the tone for the entire session. This is your first chance to show them what your team culture is all about.

Step 2: The Dynamic Warm-Up (10 Minutes)

Lead them through a dynamic warm-up that gets their bodies ready to play. This is also your first chance to evaluate athleticism. Are they coordinated? Are they focused? Are they following instructions?

Step 3: Skill Evaluation Drills (45-60 Minutes)

This is the core of your tryout. Move players through a series of drills that allow you to evaluate the key skills. Keep the drills simple and fast-paced. You want to see them get as many touches as possible.

- Passing/Serving: Start with a simple partner passing drill, then move to serving and passing. This lets you see two skills at once.
- Hitting/Setting: A simple "Queen of the Court" style hitting line is perfect. You can evaluate hitters, setters, and even defensive players all at once.

Step 4: Game-Like Play (20-30 Minutes)

This is where you see how the skills translate to a real game. Run a 6v6 scrimmage. This is your best opportunity to evaluate intangibles. Who communicates? Who leads? Who hustles? Who supports their teammates after a mistake?

Step 5: The Cool-Down and Closing (5 Minutes)

Bring all the players back together. Lead them through a light cool-down stretch. Thank them again for their hard work and effort. Clearly explain what the next steps are (e.g., "Team selections will be posted on the website tomorrow at 7 PM"). End on a positive, encouraging note. Every player should leave the gym feeling respected and appreciated, regardless of the outcome.

The Hardest Part: Making Cuts and Delivering the News

This is the part of coaching that no one likes. Making cuts is hard, but it's a necessary part of the process. Here are a few principles to guide you.

- Trust Your Gut, But Use Your Data: Your evaluation sheet provides the objective data. Your gut feeling about a player's attitude or potential is also valuable. The best decisions come from a combination of both.
- Have a Second Opinion: If you have an assistant coach or another trusted evaluator, get their input. A second set of eyes can help you see things you might have missed.
- Deliver the News with Compassion: Whether you post a list online or send emails, the way you communicate your decisions matters. If a player or parent reaches out for feedback, be prepared to give it. Be honest, be kind, and focus on specific skills they can work on. Never say, "You're just not good enough." Instead, say, "To play at this level, we need players who can consistently pass a 2.0 or higher. That's a great goal for you to work on this offseason."

Tryouts are your first, best chance to build the kind of team culture you want. When you run a tryout that is organized, fair, and positive, you send a clear message: this is a program that values not just great players but great people. And that is a team everyone wants to be part of.

SIX

Creating Your Team Culture

Now that you have your team, the real work begins. And it's probably not what you think. Before you can build a winning offense or a lockdown defense, you have to build a team. You have to build a culture.

Team culture is the invisible force that holds everything together. It's the answer to the question, "How do we do things here?" It's in the way your players talk to each other after a mistake, the way they hustle in a drill even when they're tired, and the way they carry themselves on and off the court. You can have all the talent in the world, but without a strong culture, you'll never reach your full potential.

This chapter is your guide to intentionally building a culture of respect, accountability, and connection. This is where you turn a group of individual players into a true team.

It Starts with You: The Mirror Effect

Your team's culture starts and ends with you. Your players are a mirror, reflecting the energy, attitude, and values you bring to the gym every single day. You cannot ask for respect from them if you don't show respect to the referees. You cannot ask for a positive attitude from them if you are constantly sighing with frustration on the sideline. You cannot ask for effort from them if you are not prepared and focused for practice.

Before you can build a culture, you have to be the culture. Your actions are your loudest teaching tool. If you want a team that is resilient, supportive, and hardworking, you have to model resilience, support, and hard work in everything you do.

Co-Creating Your Team Standards: The "How"

Great cultures are not built on a long list of rules handed down from the coach. They are built on a short list of standards that the team creates and agrees to together. When players have a voice in creating the standards, they are far more likely to uphold them. This is how you create buy-in.

In one of your first practices, lead your team through this simple exercise. Write these three words on a whiteboard:

- Effort
- Communication
- Respect

Then, ask your players: "What do these words look like in action? When we are at our best, what are we doing?"

Standard	What It Looks Like (Examples from a Team)
Effort	• We sprint to shag balls. • We are the first to the floor for a loose ball. • We finish every drill strong.
Communication	• We call the ball early and loudly. • We make eye contact with our teammates. • We talk to each other between plays.
Respect	• We listen when a coach or teammate is talking. • We thank our parents for driving us to practice. • We treat the other team and the referees with class.

These are not your rules; these are their standards. This is the code they have created for themselves. Now, your job is simply to help them live up to it.

The Art of Accountability: Upholding the Code

Accountability is not punishment. It is the act of holding each other to the standards you've all agreed upon. It's about creating an environment where it's safe to have hard conversations because everyone knows the goal is to make the team better.

Peer-to-Peer Accountability is the Goal

Your ultimate goal is for your players to hold each other accountable, not just you. This is the sign of a truly great team culture. But they need to be taught how. This is where you teach them the art of constructive feedback.

Teach them the "kind, specific, helpful" framework for talking to each other:

- Instead of: "You need to pass better." (Not specific or helpful).
- Try: "Hey, on that last pass, it looked like your platform was a little angled toward the outside. If you can get it angled in, I think it will go right to the target." (Kind, specific, and helpful).

When players learn how to talk to each other this way, they stop seeing feedback as criticism and start seeing it as a tool for growth.

Building Connection: The Glue That Holds It All Together

A team that is connected off the court is a team that will fight for each other on the court. Connection is the glue of a great culture. You have to be intentional about creating opportunities for your players to bond as people, not just as athletes.

Fun is Not the Enemy of Hard Work

Some coaches think that a focused practice has to be a serious practice. That's a myth. Joy is one of the most powerful motivators you have. When your players are having fun, they will work harder, learn faster, and be more resilient when things get tough.

- Inject Fun into Drills: Turn a repetitive drill into a competition. Play music during warm-ups. Let the losing team of a drill do a silly dance instead of a punishment.
- Celebrate Small Victories: Did your team finally nail a three-touch rally in a drill? Stop practice and celebrate it. High-fives, cheers, and genuine excitement are contagious.

Bonding Beyond the Court

Create opportunities for your team to connect outside of the gym. This doesn't have to be complicated or expensive.

- Team Dinners: Have a potluck at someone's house before a big tournament.

- Team Outings: Go bowling, see a movie, or do a community service project together.
- Secret Buddies: Pair up older players with younger players to be their "buddy" for the season. They can write encouraging notes, bring each other snacks, or just be a friendly face in the gym.

These small acts of connection build the trust and camaraderie that will carry your team through the inevitable challenges of a long season.

The Heart of Culture

Your team culture is the legacy you will leave long after the season is over. Your players may not remember the exact score of every game, but they will remember how it felt to be a part of your team. They will remember if they felt respected, supported, and challenged. They will remember if they learned how to be a good teammate.

Culture isn't built in a day. It's built in a thousand small moments—in the way you greet your players at the door, the way you respond to a mistake, and the way you celebrate their effort. Be intentional about those moments, and you will build a culture that everyone is proud to be a part of.

SEVEN

Teaching the Basics: Essential Skills to Master Early

Welcome to the heart of on-court coaching. This is where you translate your philosophy and your season plan into actual, tangible skill development. But great coaching isn't just about knowing the skills; it's about knowing how to teach them. And modern coaching science has shown us that how we teach is just as important as what we teach.

This chapter is your guide to teaching the most critical skills your team needs to master early: passing, serving, and the fundamental movement patterns that make everything else possible. We'll do it using principles from motor learning—the science of how athletes actually acquire skills—to make your coaching more efficient, more effective, and a lot more fun.

The Golden Rule of Skill Development: Practice Must Look Like the Game

If you take only one thing from this chapter, let it be this: players learn fastest when practice looks like the game. This is the principle of specificity. If you want your players to get better at passing a real serve in a real game, they need to practice passing real serves in real, game-like situations. Drills that are too perfect, too predictable, or too controlled don't transfer to the beautiful chaos of a real match.

Your goal is not to create players who look great in neat, orderly drills. Your goal is to create players who can solve the messy problems that volleyball presents on every single play. That means your drills should be built around three things: reading, deciding, and doing.

Skill #1: Passing - The Foundation of Everything

No skill is more important than passing. You can't run an offense without a good pass. It is the foundation upon which your entire team is built. Here's how to teach it effectively.

The Goal: Create a consistent, accurate first contact that gets the ball to the target area.

The Common Mistake: Coaches often break passing down into too many small, isolated parts (e.g., "freeze your platform," "hold your finish"). This creates robotic players who can't adapt.

The Better Way: Teach the Whole Skill with External Cues

Instead of focusing on body parts, give your players simple, external goals. Their brains will organize the movement for them.

Skill Component	Common Internal Cue (Less Effective)	Better External Cue (More Effective)
Platform	"Lock your elbows."	"Show the server a big, quiet surfboard."
Footwork	"Move your feet to the ball."	"Beat the ball to the spot."
Angle	"Angle your platform to the target."	"Aim your surfboard at the setter's window."

A Simple, Game-Like Passing Progression:

1. Coach Toss to Passer: The coach tosses a simple, predictable ball. The passer's only job is to get the ball to a target (a cone, a hoop, or a person).
2. Player Toss to Passer: Now, a player tosses the ball. This adds a small amount of variability.
3. Player Serves to Passer: A player serves from a short distance. Now the passer has to read a real serve.
4. Serve, Pass, Set: Add a setter. The passer's job is now to get the ball to a moving target.
5. Serve, Pass, Set, Hit: Add a hitter. Now the pass initiates a full offensive play.

Notice how each step gets closer to a real game? That's how you build skills that transfer.

Skill #2: Serving - The First Weapon

Serving is the only skill in volleyball that you have complete control over. It is your team's first and best weapon. A tough serve can win you points outright and take the other team completely out of their offense.

The Goal: Create a consistent, tough serve that puts pressure on the other team.

The Common Mistake: Spending too much time on serving form in a static line, with no pressure and no target.

The Better Way: Make Serving a Competitive, Goal-Oriented Skill

From day one, serving should be practiced with a clear target and a clear goal. This turns a boring drill into a fun, competitive game.

Skill Component	Common Internal Cue (Less Effective)	Better External Cue (More Effective)
Toss	"Toss the ball to the right height."	"Toss the ball to a spot just above your hitting shoulder."
Contact	"Snap your wrist."	"Drive your hand through the middle of the ball."
Follow-Through	"Follow through to your opposite hip."	"Follow your hand all the way to your pocket."

A Simple, Game-Like Serving Progression:

1. Target Practice: Place targets (cones, towels, or even just numbers on a whiteboard) in different zones on the other side of the court. Challenge players to hit specific zones.
2. Serving for Points: Turn serving into a game. Give players 3 points for an ace, 1 point for a serve that the other team can't attack, and -1 point for a missed serve. This teaches them to balance aggressiveness with consistency.
3. Serve and Play: The most game-like drill of all. A player serves, and the point is played out. This forces them to transition immediately from serving to playing defense.

Skill #3: Movement - The Invisible Skill

Great volleyball players are not just skilled; they are great movers. They are balanced, efficient, and always ready to move in any direction. You should be teaching movement patterns in every single drill you run.

The Goal: Develop athletic, balanced, and efficient movement patterns.

The Common Mistake: Treating agility drills (ladders, cones) as a separate part of practice. Movement should be integrated into your volleyball drills.

The Better Way: Focus on Two Key Movement Patterns

1. The "Ready" Position: This is the foundation of all movement. Players should be in a balanced, athletic stance before the ball is served. Cues like "be ready to pounce" or "be light on your feet" are more effective than "bend your knees."
2. The First Step: The first step is the most important. It should be quick, explosive, and in the right direction. Instead of telling players to "be faster," give them a specific cue like, "Can your first step beat the ball to the spot?"

How to Integrate Movement Into Drills:

- In any passing drill, make sure the player has to move to the ball. Don't toss it right at them.
- In any hitting drill, make sure the player transitions off the net and then starts their approach.
- In any defensive drill, make sure the player starts in a ready position and reacts to a hitter.

Simple Game IQ: Helping Your Players See the Game

Game IQ is about understanding the "why" behind the skills. It's about seeing the game, not just playing it. You can start teaching simple game IQ from the very first practice.

The Goal: Help players understand the basic flow and objectives of the game.

The Common Mistake: Overloading young players with complex strategic concepts.

The Better Way: Focus on One Simple Concept at a Time

- Better the Ball: The goal of every contact is to make the ball better for your teammate. A passer's job is to make the setter's job easier. A setter's job is to make the hitter's job easier. This simple concept teaches teamwork and purpose.
- Three Contacts: Teach your team that the goal is always to get three contacts on the ball. This prevents them from panicking and sending over a free ball on the first or second touch.

- Home Base: Teach every player a "home base" position they should return to after every play. This gives them a sense of structure and prevents them from getting lost on the court.

Putting It All Together: Your First Practice

Your first few practices are all about building a foundation. Don't worry about complex drills or advanced strategies. Focus on high-rep, game-like drills that teach the fundamentals of passing, serving, and movement. Keep it fun, keep it positive, and keep it moving.

Remember the golden rule: if it doesn't look like volleyball, it's probably not making your players better at volleyball. Build your practices around the beautiful, chaotic, and problem-solving nature of the game, and you will build players who are ready for anything.

EIGHT

Building Mental Toughness: The Four Pillars

Mental toughness isn't about trying to look unbothered or pretending you never feel upset. It's not about forcing yourself to "be strong" or pushing emotions down. Real toughness in volleyball simply means this: staying connected to your goals even when something hard happens.

Every athlete faces moments that shake them a bit—a missed serve, a rough rotation, a coach's correction, a teammate misunderstanding, a noisy gym, or a stressful week off the court. None of these moments make you weak. They make you human. Mental toughness is not about avoiding hard moments; it's about how you respond to them. And the best news? It's not a personality trait. It's a skill. Which means you can train it just like passing, serving, or movement.

Mental toughness grows in four layers: tolerance, fortitude, resilience, and adaptability. When athletes learn what each layer looks like on the court, they gain a language for understanding their own reactions—and a roadmap for improving them.

Tolerance is the ability to stay steady before something rattles your behavior. Some players get thrown off by a single mistake or a single correction. Others stay composed through multiple challenges before emotions start taking the steering wheel. Tolerance doesn't mean ignoring your feelings; it simply means noticing frustration without immediately acting on it. Athletes with growing tolerance stay present longer, think more clearly, and keep choosing good decisions even when the pressure rises. This skill grows when players pause in the moment they start slipping and give themselves a breath to settle back into their intention.

Fortitude shows up the moment something does get to you. Everyone hits a breaking point eventually; that's normal. The question is: how big is the dip? Some athletes spiral quickly—shoulders drop, body language collapses, communication disappears, or they turn inward. Others still feel the sting, but their behavior only dips a little: a breath, a quick shake-off, and they rejoin the moment without damaging themselves or the team. Fortitude isn't about never cracking. It's about the size of the wobble when you do. As soon as athletes start recognizing their own patterns—"this is when I fall hard"—they gain the control to soften that drop next time.

Resilience is how long it takes to come back. This is the part most young players struggle with. One mistake becomes five. A rough drill ruins the whole practice. A single rotation becomes a black hole of self-doubt. Resilience is the speed of your rebound—the time between "ouch" and "I'm back." High resilience doesn't mean you don't feel affected. It means you recover quickly enough that the moment doesn't control your entire day. With practice, players go from needing twenty minutes to reset, down to ten, then five, then a few breaths between points. This is the quiet magic of mental toughness: learning to shorten the slump.

Adaptability is the long-term effect of a tough moment. After something hard happens, do you become stronger, stay the same, or carry more fear? High adaptability means challenges leave you wiser, more confident, and more self-aware. Medium adaptability means you return to your old baseline without much change. Low adaptability means the experience makes you more fragile—avoiding the ball, doubting yourself, shrinking in tough moments. The goal isn't perfection; it's learning to ask, "What can this teach me?" in a realistic, grounded way. Even uncomfortable moments can become turning points when framed with curiosity instead of fear.

Picture a player named Emma. She's serving at 20–22. She misses long and immediately shuts down for the rest of the set. Her tolerance held until the highest-pressure moment. Her fortitude dipped sharply. Her resilience was slow—she never recovered during the set. And her adaptability suffered—she told herself she never wanted to serve again. Now imagine Emma a month later, after training mental toughness: she misses a serve, takes one breath, relaxes her shoulders, reconnects with her teammates, plays fully on the next point, and asks to practice serving after training. That's growth in all four areas. That's what mental toughness looks like in real life—small improvements layered over time, built through awareness and repetition.

To train these skills, athletes don't need dramatic speeches or motivational slogans. They need simple, practical habits. The first is micro-resets: one breath between points, one shoulder shake, one clear thought like "next ball." These tiny routines anchor the mind. The second is controlled recovery: after a mistake, take three seconds to exhale, return to steady body language, make brief eye contact with a teammate, and re-engage. The third is challenge rehearsal: practicing intentionally in hard situations, like serving under pressure or playing while fatigued, so tough moments feel familiar rather than frightening. The fourth is reframing: instead of letting a mistake define you, ask how it might help you grow. And finally, the most powerful habit: choosing behavior over feelings. You're allowed to feel anything—frustration, embarrassment, pressure—but you don't have to let those feelings dictate how you act.

Mental toughness isn't loud or dramatic. It's quiet, steady, and deeply practical. It looks like noticing when you're shaken, recovering faster than before, falling less dramatically, learning from challenges, and continuing to choose actions that support your goals. No athlete does this perfectly, and no one needs to. But with practice, every athlete can become someone who stays composed in chaos, recovers quickly from mistakes, and grows stronger through adversity. That—steady, intentional growth—is the heart of true mental toughness.

NINE

Your First Practices: Structure, Warmups, and Early Teaching Cues

The day is finally here. Your clipboard is ready, your whistle is around your neck, and a gym full of excited, nervous players is looking at you. Welcome to your first practice. This is where your season truly begins. The goal of your first few practices is not perfection; it's to set a positive trajectory. It's about building a foundation of good habits, clear communication, and a culture of fun, focused energy.

This chapter is your roadmap for those crucial first few sessions. We'll cover the simple structure of a great practice, how to run a warm-up with purpose, the essential communication cues you'll use all season, and a sample practice plan you can use for your very first day.

The Anatomy of a Great Practice: A Simple 5-Part Structure

A well-structured practice flows naturally from one segment to the next, keeps players engaged, and maximizes learning. Don't overcomplicate it. A great 90-minute practice can be broken down into five simple parts.

1. The Welcome & Dynamic Warm-Up (15 minutes): This is where you set the tone. It's not just about getting bodies warm; it's about getting minds focused and connected.
2. Skill #1 Focus (20 minutes): Dedicate a focused block of time to one primary skill (e.g., passing).
3. Skill #2 Focus or Combination (20 minutes): Work on a second skill (e.g., serving) or a drill that combines the first skill with a second (e.g., serve-pass).
4. Game-Like Play (25 minutes): This is where the learning gets locked in. Put the skills to work in a competitive, game-like context.
5. The Cool-Down & Closing (10 minutes): Bring the energy down, stretch, and end practice with a clear, positive message.

The Purposeful Warm-Up: More Than Just Jogging

The warm-up is one of the most valuable and underutilized parts of practice. It's not just a time to prevent injury; it's your first opportunity to teach, connect, and set the standard for the day. A purposeful warm-up has three goals:

- Movement Prep: Get the muscles warm and the body ready to move explosively.
- Skill Activation: Get players touching the ball in a low-pressure, high-rep way.
- Mental Engagement: Get their minds focused and ready to learn.

A Simple, Purposeful Warm-Up (15 minutes):

- Dynamic Movement (5 mins): Start with dynamic movements like high knees, butt kicks, lunges, and arm circles. Keep it moving and energetic.
- Partner Passing (5 mins): Have players partner up and do simple, controlled passing. The focus is on quality touches, not intensity.
- Team Huddle (5 mins): Bring the team in. Briefly state the "one thing" you're focusing on in practice today (e.g., "Today, we are going to be great at communicating on every single play").

This gives the practice a clear purpose.

Early Teaching Cues: Your Communication Toolkit

Clear, consistent communication is your coaching superpower. In the heat of a drill, players can't process long sentences. You need a toolkit of short, memorable, external cues that tell them exactly what to do. This is called "Teaching in Keys." You're giving them one key thought to unlock the right movement.

Here are some essential cues to introduce in your first practices:

Skill	Your Go-To Cue	What It Means
Passing	"Beat the ball to the spot."	Focuses on early footwork, not just reaching with the arms.
Serving	"Hand to target."	Encourages a full follow-through in the direction of the serve.
Setting	"Finish like Superman."	Promotes holding the follow-through, which creates consistency.
Hitting	"High elbow, fast arm."	A simple reminder for the two most important parts of the arm swing.
Communication	"Call it by name!"	Instead of just "I got it," players should call the ball with their name: "Lexi! Lexi! Lexi!" It's clearer and more confident.

Introduce these cues on day one. Use them consistently. Write them on your whiteboard. Soon, they will become the shared language of your team.

The Power of Clarity: Tell Them How Long

Here's a coaching principle that seems small but makes an enormous difference: always tell your players how long each drill will last. Think about the last time you went to a movie theater without knowing how long the film was. You'd be checking your watch constantly, wondering when it would end, unable to fully settle in and enjoy the experience. Your players feel the same way in practice. When they don't know how long a drill lasts, part of their brain is always wondering, "When is this going to be over?" instead of being fully committed to the task. But when you say, "We're doing this drill for exactly 8 minutes," something shifts. They know the finish line. They can pace their energy. They can fully commit to those 8 minutes knowing there's a clear endpoint. This simple act of transparency removes the mental fog and allows them to focus entirely on the work. It also teaches them respect for time and structure—two things that will serve them well both on and off the court. So before every drill, announce the duration. "We're going to do target serving for 10 minutes. Go!" It takes two seconds, but it changes everything about how your players engage.

Your First Practice Plan: A 90-Minute Sample

Here is a simple, effective practice plan you can use for your very first day. It's designed to be fun, fast-paced, and focused on the fundamentals.

PRACTICE #1: BUILDING THE FOUNDATION

- Theme: Great Effort & Communication
- Welcome & Dynamic Warm-Up (0-15 mins):
- Welcome the team, share your excitement for the season.
- Dynamic warm-up, followed by partner passing.
- Team Huddle: "Our focus today is simple: we will give great effort and communicate on every play."
- Skill #1: Passing (15-35 mins)
- Drill: Pass to a Target. The coach tosses balls to players, who have to pass to a cone or a coach.

Focus on the cue: "Beat the ball to the spot."

- Skill #2: Serving (35-55 mins)
- Drill: Target Serving. Place targets in different zones. Players serve to hit the targets. Focus on the cue: "Hand to target."
- Game-Like Play (55-80 mins)
- Game: Serve & Play 3v3. A server serves to a team of three passers. The passers must try to get three contacts. This is a simple, game-like drill that combines both skills you just worked on.
- Cool-Down & Closing (80-90 mins)
- Light stretching.
- Closing Huddle: Ask the players: "What's one thing you learned today?" or "Who was a great teammate today and why?" End with a positive message and a team cheer.

Setting Expectations on Day One

Your first practice is also your first opportunity to establish your team standards. This isn't about reading a long list of rules; it's about showing them what your culture looks like in action.

- Expect Effort: When a ball is shanked, is your first reaction to praise the player who hustled to try and save it? That shows that you value effort over perfection.
- Expect Communication: When the gym is quiet, are you the one bringing the energy and reminding them to talk? That shows that communication is a non-negotiable.
- Expect Respect: Do you make eye contact with every player? Do you listen when they ask a question? That shows them what respect looks like.

Your first practice sets the trajectory for your entire season. Don't worry about getting everything perfect. Focus on bringing positive energy, communicating clearly, and making every player feel seen and valued. If you do that, you've already won.

PART III
Managing the Season

TEN

Your First Games: What to Expect

The gym is louder, the lights are brighter, and there's a team on the other side of the net that you haven't seen before. Welcome to your first game. All the practice, all the planning—it all leads to this. It's normal to feel a mix of excitement and nerves. Your players are feeling it, too. Your job on game day is not to be a perfect strategist; it's to be a calm, steady leader who helps your team navigate the beautiful chaos of competition.

This chapter is your guide to managing your first games. We'll cover your role on the sideline, how to create a positive and engaged bench, a simple approach to substitutions and timeouts, and a communication system that will keep your team focused and confident.

Your Three Roles on Game Day: The Coach's Sideline Hats

During a game, you'll wear three different hats. Knowing which hat to wear and when is the art of sideline coaching.

1. The Observer: Your primary job is to see the game. What is the other team doing? Where are they serving? Who is our weakest passer right now? Who is struggling with their confidence? You can't make good decisions if you're not gathering good information. Stay calm, stay observant, and trust what you see.
2. The Strategist: Based on what you observe, you make small, simple adjustments. This is not the time for complex new plays. It's about making small tweaks to your existing game plan. If the other team has a hot hitter, you might adjust your block. If your server is on a roll, you might have them target a specific player. Keep it simple.
3. The Stabilizer: This is your most important role. Your team will look to you to gauge how they should be feeling. If you are calm, they will be calm. If you are frantic, they will be frantic. Your body language, your tone of voice, and your presence on the sideline are your most powerful coaching tools. You are the emotional anchor of the team.

The Bench: Your Team's "Learning Zone"

The players on the bench are not just waiting to play; they are part of the team. A positive, engaged bench is a huge competitive advantage. From day one, establish that the bench is a "Learning Zone," not a waiting room. Players on the bench have three important jobs:

- Job #1: Be a Great Teammate: Cheer for your teammates on the court. Celebrate good plays. Offer encouragement after a mistake. A loud, positive bench can completely change the energy of a game.
- Job #2: Be a Student of the Game: Watch the other team. Where are their best hitters? Who is their weakest passer? When a player comes off the court, they should be able to tell their teammate who is replacing them what they saw. This keeps them engaged and makes them smarter players.
- Job #3: Be Ready: A player can be called into the game at any moment. They need to be mentally and physically ready to go. This means they are paying attention to the game, they know the score, and they are ready to contribute the second their number is called.

A Simple Philosophy for Substitutions

Substitutions can be stressful, especially for new coaches. Don't overcomplicate it. For your first season, your substitution philosophy should be guided by two simple principles:

1. Give Opportunities: In youth volleyball, development is more important than winning. Your goal should be to get as many players into the game as you can, especially in the early part of the season. This keeps players engaged and gives them valuable game-time experience.
2. Sub with a Purpose: When you do make a sub, have a clear reason. Are you subbing in a better server to try and score a few points? Are you subbing in a defensive specialist to shore up your back row? Or are you subbing a player who is struggling emotionally to give them a moment to reset? Know your "why."

Timeouts: Your 60-Second Reset Button

Timeouts are your most powerful tool for managing the momentum and emotional state of a game. Don't wait until you're down by 10 points to call one. Use your timeouts strategically to achieve one of three goals:

- Goal #1: To Break the Other Team's Momentum. If the other team has scored 3-4 points in a row, call a timeout. It doesn't even matter what you say. The act of stopping the game, giving your team a breather, and forcing the other server to think about their next serve is often enough to break the run.
- Goal #2: To Give One, Simple Instruction. Your players can only process one, maybe two, pieces of information in a timeout. Don't overwhelm them. Pick one simple thing you want them to focus on. "They are tipping to zone 4. Let's be ready for it." Or, "We are playing great defense. Now let's make sure we are taking aggressive swings."
- Goal #3: To Reset Your Team's Energy. Sometimes, you just need to bring your team in, take a deep breath, and remind them to have fun. If they look frantic or scared, use your timeout to be a calming presence. "Hey, we're okay. Let's take a breath. Go out there and have fun."

In-Game Communication System: Simple, Positive, and Actionable

Your communication during a game should be like a series of clear, positive headlines, not long, complicated paragraphs. Here is a simple system for in-game communication.

Communication Type	What It Is	Examples
The Positive Reinforcer	A quick, positive comment that reinforces a good play or effort.	"Great hustle, Sarah!" "That's the way to talk, team!" "Awesome swing, Maria!"
The "Feed-Forward" Cue	A simple, future-focused instruction that tells a player what to do next, without dwelling on the mistake.	Instead of "You were late on that block," try, "Next time, let's see if you can get your hands over just a split second earlier."
The Team-Wide Reminder	A short, clear reminder to the whole team about one of your key principles.	"Hey, let's make sure we're talking on every play!" "Remember, aggressive swings!"

The Post-Game Huddle: Win or Lose

Your post-game huddle should be the same whether you won by 10 or lost by 10. This is your last chance to reinforce your team's culture. Keep it short, keep it positive, and focus on the things you can control.

- Acknowledge Effort: "I am so proud of the way you all fought for every single point today."
- Highlight a Positive: "Our communication in that second set was the best it's been all season."
- Share a Lesson: "We learned today that we need to be more aggressive with our out-of-system swings. That's what we'll work on in practice this week."

Game day is a learning experience—for your players and for you. Don't expect to be a perfect coach in your first game. Expect to learn, expect to grow, and most importantly, expect to have fun. Your players will follow your lead.

ELEVEN

Tournament Survival Guide

A single game is a sprint, but a tournament is a full marathon. It's a long, emotional, high-energy day packed with big highs, tough lows, and more waiting around than you'd ever expect. For a new coach, the whole thing can feel a bit like trying to conduct an orchestra in the middle of a storm. But with a plan, a steady mindset, and a backpack full of the right essentials, you won't just survive your first tournament—you'll actually enjoy it.

Not all coaches face marathon-style days, but many do. In tournament play, it's normal to have multiple matches back-to-back with only short breaks in between. You might battle through a long three-set match… and then find yourself warming up for the next one twenty minutes later. That's why tournament days require a completely different approach than a regular game day. The pace, energy management, emotions, and recovery all change.

This chapter is your guide through it all. You'll find simple, practical strategies for navigating every part of a tournament day—warm-ups, nutrition, downtime, emotions, team rhythm, and even the parents who get more nervous than the athletes. With the right mindset and a little preparation, tournament days become some of the most rewarding coaching experiences you'll ever have.

The Marathon Mindset: It's All About Energy

Success in a tournament is not about playing perfect volleyball all day. It's about managing energy—physical, mental, and emotional. The team with the most energy left in the championship match is often the one that wins. Your job as the coach is to be the master of energy conservation for your entire team, including yourself.

Before the First Whistle: Your Arrival Plan

A smooth start sets the tone for the entire day. Your arrival plan should be simple and clear.

- Arrival Time: Have your team arrive 45-60 minutes before your first match. This

gives them plenty of time to check in, get their bearings, and warm up without feeling rushed.
- The Team Huddle: Before you even touch a ball, gather your team. Set one simple, positive intention for the day. Not "Let's win," but something like, "Today, we are going to be the best teammates on and off the court."
- The Tournament Warm-Up: A tournament warm-up is different from a practice warm-up. It needs to be shorter, more efficient, and focused on getting players game-ready quickly. A simple 20-minute warm-up works perfectly:
- Dynamic Movement (5 mins): High knees, butt kicks, lunges, arm circles.
- Partner Pepper (10 mins): Simple, controlled passing, setting, and hitting with a partner.
- Team Serving (5 mins): A few serves to get the arm warm and the nerves out.

Managing the Day: A Coach's Guide to the Grind

Tournaments are full of challenges that don't show up in a regular game. Here's how to handle them.

Challenge	Your Survival Strategy
Long Breaks Between Matches	This is where teams lose their energy. To stay strong, you need a clear plan. That's where the 3 R's come in: Rest (find a quiet spot for the team to sit), Refuel (this is the time for a healthy snack), and Relax (encourage players to listen to music, chat with friends, or do anything that gets their mind off volleyball for a bit).
Player Nutrition & Hydration	You can't control what your players eat, but you can educate them. Send a note to parents before the tournament with simple guidelines: pack lots of water, avoid sugary drinks, and bring healthy snacks like fruit, granola bars, and pretzels. A player fueled by candy will crash by the third match.
Managing Nerves (Theirs & Yours)	Nerves are normal. The goal isn't to eliminate them; it's to manage them. Teach your players the "Anchor Breath" (inhale for 4, hold for 4, exhale for 4). When you see a player getting nervous, don't say, "Don't be nervous." Say, "Let's take one good breath together." And remember to use your own internal traffic light. Your calmness is their anchor.
Managing Parents	Parents get nervous, too. Before the tournament, send a reminder about your 24-hour rule and encourage them to be a source of positive energy. If a parent approaches you during the tournament with a concern, have a polite, prepared response: "I really appreciate you wanting to talk. For the sake of the team, my focus has to be on the players right now. Can we schedule a time to chat tomorrow?"

The Match-to-Match Reset: The 10-Minute Rule

What you do in the 10 minutes after a match is more important than what you do in the 10 minutes before the next one. Win or lose, your post-match routine should be the same. This creates emotional stability and helps your team reset and refocus. I call it the "10-Minute Rule."

1. Find Your Space (2 minutes): As soon as the match ends, lead your team away from the court to a quiet spot. This creates a physical and mental separation from the game.
2. One Positive, One to Grow On (3 minutes): Keep the post-game talk short and simple. Your players are tired and can't process a lot of information. Start with one specific, genuine positive. "The way we covered our hitters in that last set was the best it's been all season." Then, offer one simple thing to focus on for the next match. "In our next match, let's focus on making our first contact a little higher."
3. Let It Go (5 minutes): This is the most important step. After you've had your quick chat, officially release them from the game. Say the words: "Okay, that game is over. Let it go. Go get some water, have a snack, and be ready to warm up for our next match in 30 minutes." This gives them permission to mentally move on.

The Heart of the Tournament

A successful tournament is not measured in wins and losses; it's measured in resilience. Did your team handle adversity with grace? Did they support each other when they were tired and frustrated? Did they represent your program with class? If the answer is yes, then you've had a winning day, no matter what the scoreboard says.

Your job as the coach is to guide them through that journey. Stay calm, stay positive, and keep your sense of humor. And don't forget to pack your own snacks. You're going to need them, too.

TWELVE

Mid-Season Reflection & Adjustments

You've made it to the halfway point of the season. You've survived your first practices, your first games, and your first tournament. You've seen your team at their best and at their most frustrated. The middle of the season is the perfect time to pause, reflect, and make the small, smart adjustments that will set your team up for a strong finish.

This is not about reinventing the wheel; it's about fine-tuning the engine. This chapter is your guide to the mid-season reset: how to track your team's progress, how to correct course when things aren't working, how to navigate the inevitable mid-season slump, and how to keep your players motivated for the home stretch.

The Mid-Season Check-In: Are We Where We Thought We'd Be?

Remember that "North Star" objective you set back in Chapter 4? Now is the time to pull it out. The most important question you can ask yourself at the mid-season point is not "What is our record?" but "Are we on track to achieve our North Star?"

Take 30 minutes with a notebook and ask yourself these three questions:

1. What's working? What are our biggest strengths right now? Is it our serving? Our team chemistry? Our defensive effort? Identify what's going well and celebrate it. Make a plan to do more of it.
2. What's not working? Where are we struggling? Is it our serve receive? Our out-of-system offense? Our energy on the bench? Be honest with yourself. This is not about blame; it's about identifying problems so you can start solving them.
3. What one or two things could we focus on to make the biggest impact? You can't fix everything at once. Pick one or two key areas that will give you the most bang for your buck. Maybe it's dedicating an extra 10 minutes of every practice to serve receive. Maybe it's having a team meeting to talk about communication. Small, focused changes are more effective than trying to overhaul everything at once.

Tracking Progress: Beyond Wins and Losses

It's easy to get caught up in your win-loss record. But that number doesn't tell the whole story. A better way to track your team's progress is to focus on the things you can actually control. Here are a few simple metrics you can track to get a clearer picture of your team's growth.

Metric	What It Measures	How to Track It
First Ball Side-Out %	How often you win the point when you serve receive. This is the single most important stat in volleyball.	For every 10 serves your team receives in a match, how many times did you win the point?
Serving %	How often your serves go in the court.	Track aces, in-play serves, and errors. Are you being aggressive but inconsistent? Or too safe?
Three-Contact %	How often your team gets three contacts on the ball before sending it over.	This is a great measure of your team's ball control and composure.

You don't need complex software. A simple tally on a clipboard will do. Tracking these numbers will help you see if the things you're working on in practice are actually showing up in games.

Navigating the Mid-Season Slump: It's Normal

Every team, at every level, goes through a mid-season slump. The season is long. Players are tired. The initial excitement has worn off. It's normal. Your job is not to prevent the slump, but to lead your team through it. Here are a few strategies.

- Change the Scenery: Break up the monotony. Have a practice at a park or a sand court. Play a different sport for a day. Sometimes, a simple change of environment is all it takes to reset the energy.
- Inject Fun: Double down on the fun. Have a theme day at practice (e.g., crazy sock day). Play more games and fewer structured drills. Remember, joy is a powerful motivator.
- Go Back to Basics: Sometimes a slump is a sign that your team's fundamental foundation is cracking. Spend a practice or two going back to the basics of passing, serving, and footwork. This can help rebuild their confidence.

Keeping Players Motivated: The Power of "Why"

By the middle of the season, some of your players might be struggling with motivation, especially those who aren't getting a lot of playing time. This is where you, as the coach, need to reconnect them to their "why."

- Individual Check-Ins: Take a few minutes before or after practice to check in with each player individually. Ask them simple questions: "How are you feeling about the season?" "What's one thing you're proud of so far?" "What's one thing you want to work on?" These small conversations show that you care about them as people, not just as players.
- Redefine Roles: For players who aren't playing a lot, give them a new, important role. Maybe they are the "bench captain," in charge of leading the cheers. Maybe they are the "stat master," in charge of tracking a specific stat during games. Giving them a sense of purpose can be a powerful motivator.
- Connect Back to the North Star: Remind the team of the north star objective you all set at the beginning of the season. Are you trying to be the most resilient team in the gym? Are you trying to be the best teammates you can be? Reconnecting them to that shared purpose can help them see beyond their individual frustrations.

The Coach's Mid-Season Reset

Finally, don't forget to do a mid-season reset for yourself. You're probably tired, too. Take a night off. Go see a movie. Read a book that has nothing to do with volleyball. You cannot pour from an empty cup. Your team needs you to be energized and engaged for the home stretch. Take care of yourself so you can take care of them.

The middle of the season is where great teams are forged. It's not about being perfect; it's about being willing to reflect, adjust, and grow. Embrace the challenge, and you'll set your team up for a finish they can be proud of.

THIRTEEN

Burnout Prevention & Emotional Support

As a coach, you are more than just a strategist. You are a leader, a mentor, and often, a primary source of emotional support for your players. The modern youth athlete faces tremendous pressure—from school, social media, parents, and themselves. A long, grueling season can take a toll on their physical and mental well-being. Your ability to recognize the signs of burnout and create a psychologically safe environment is one of the most important and impactful parts of your job.

This chapter is your guide to becoming a coach who supports the whole athlete. We'll cover how to spot and prevent burnout, how to help players navigate confidence issues, and how to build a team culture where it's safe to be vulnerable.

The Coach's Role: You Are a First Responder, Not a Therapist

This is the most important principle in this chapter. It is not your job to be a mental health professional. You are not trained or qualified to diagnose or treat mental health issues. Your role is to be a caring, observant, and supportive first responder. You are there to notice when a player is struggling, to create a safe space for them to talk, and to connect them with the appropriate resources (like their parents or a school counselor) if necessary. Know your role, and know your limits.

Burnout: The Silent Opponent

Burnout is a state of physical, emotional, and mental exhaustion caused by prolonged stress. It's not the same as just being tired. It's a deeper, more persistent feeling of depletion. In athletes, it often shows up in a few key ways:

- Physical Signs: Persistent muscle soreness, frequent minor injuries, a decline in performance, or looking chronically tired.
- Emotional Signs: Increased irritability, a negative or cynical attitude, a loss of joy or passion for the sport, or seeming withdrawn from teammates.

How to Prevent Burnout: The Power of Proactive Rest

The best way to deal with burnout is to prevent it from happening in the first place. This is where you, as the coach, have significant control.

Prevention Strategy	What It Looks Like in Practice
Schedule "Off" Days	Intentionally schedule days off in your season calendar, especially after a long tournament. This shows your players that rest is a priority.
Vary Your Practice Intensity	Not every practice has to be a grind. Plan for a mix of high-intensity and low-intensity days. A light, fun, skills-focused practice can be just as valuable as a tough, competitive one.
Listen to Their Bodies (and Their Minds)	Create a culture where it's okay for players to say, "Coach, I'm feeling really run down today." This doesn't mean they get a free pass, but it gives you important information. Maybe you adjust their reps for the day, or maybe you just check in with them to see how they're doing.

The Confidence Rollercoaster: Supporting Players Through Slumps

Every player, no matter how talented, will go through a crisis of confidence. They'll have a bad game, get into a serving slump, or just feel like they can't do anything right. How you respond in these moments can make all the difference.

The Confidence Killers (What to Avoid):

- Vague, negative feedback: "You're playing terribly today."
- Over-coaching: Trying to fix ten things at once.
- Comparing them to other players: "Why can't you pass like Sarah?"

The Confidence Builders (What to Do Instead):

- Remind them of their strengths: When a player is in a slump, they forget everything they're good at. Be the voice that reminds them. "Hey, I know you're struggling with your serve right now, but your defense has been incredible today."
- Focus on one, small, achievable goal: Give them one simple thing to focus on. "For

the next five minutes, I just want you to focus on having a great, consistent toss." This gives them a small win they can build on.

Psychological Safety: The Foundation of a Resilient Team

Psychological safety is the shared belief that it is safe to take interpersonal risks on a team. It's the feeling that you can be yourself, make mistakes, and speak up without fear of punishment or humiliation. It is the absolute bedrock of a healthy, resilient team culture.

How to Build Psychological Safety:

1. Your Reaction to Mistakes is Everything: When a player makes a mistake in a big moment, what is your first reaction? Do you throw your hands up in frustration? Or do you make eye contact, give them a nod of encouragement, and say, "Hey, we're okay. Next ball." Your players are watching. Your reaction tells them whether it's safe to fail.
2. Separate the Person from the Performance: A player is not their performance. They are a person who had a bad game. Make sure your feedback reflects this. Instead of "You were terrible today," try, "That wasn't your best game, but I know you'll bounce back. What's one thing we can work on in practice this week to help you feel more confident?"
3. Encourage Player Voice: Create opportunities for players to share their thoughts and feelings. This could be in a team meeting, in an individual check-in, or even through an anonymous survey. When players feel like their voice matters, they feel more connected to the team and more invested in its success.

The Coach's Mandate

Supporting your players' emotional well-being is not a "soft" skill; it is a core competency of great coaching. A team that feels supported, connected, and safe is a team that will be more resilient, more confident, and ultimately, more successful. You are not just coaching volleyball players; you are coaching young people. And the lessons they learn from you about how to handle adversity, how to support each other, and how to be a good teammate will last long after their playing days are over.

PART IV
Advanced Coaching Flow

FOURTEEN

Running Competitive, High-Energy Practices

As your team progresses, your practices need to evolve, too. The foundational drills of the early season give way to a new challenge: preparing your team for the speed, pressure, and intensity of real competition. This is where you, the coach, become a master of energy. A great late-season practice is not just about working hard; it's about working smart. It's about knowing when to push the tempo, when to slow down and teach, and how to create an environment that is as mentally and physically demanding as a real match.

This chapter is your guide to running competitive, high-energy practices. We'll cover the art of managing practice intensity, the power of competitive drills, and the secret to integrating conditioning seamlessly into your skill work.

The Practice Dial: Knowing When to Push and When to Teach

Think of your practice intensity as a dial that you can turn up or down. It's not always set to 10. The art of coaching is knowing when to turn the dial up to create pressure and competition, and when to turn it down to focus on learning and technique. A great practice has a rhythm, a natural flow between high-intensity and low-intensity moments.

Dial Setting	The Goal	What It Looks Like in Practice
Low (The "Teaching Zone")	This is for learning a new skill or refining a complex movement. The focus is on quality reps, not speed or outcome.	You're stopping to give feedback, players are asking questions, and the pace is slower and more deliberate.
Medium (The "Repetition Zone")	This is for getting a high volume of quality reps of a skill that players already understand. The pace is faster, but the focus is still on execution, not just winning or losing.	A fast-paced passing drill where the goal is to get as many good contacts as possible.
High (The "Competition Zone")	This is for simulating the pressure of a real game. The focus is on competing, problem-solving, and performing under pressure.	A 6v6 scrimmage where you are keeping score, and there is a consequence for the losing team (e.g., 10 push-ups).

A great practice will move between these zones. You might start in the Teaching Zone to introduce a new concept, move to the Repetition Zone to get some reps, and then finish in the Competition Zone to see if the skill holds up under pressure.

The Power of Competition: Why Keeping Score Matters

As we learned in the motor learning chapter, practice needs to look like the game. And in a game, there is always a winner and a loser. Adding a competitive element to your drills is one of the most powerful ways to increase focus, effort, and transfer of skills to a real match. When players are competing, they are not just going through the motions; they are problem-solving, communicating, and learning to handle pressure.

How to Make Any Drill Competitive

- Keep Score: The simplest way to add competition. The first team to 10 points wins.
- Add a Consequence: The losing team has a small, manageable consequence (e.g., they have to shag the balls for the next drill). This raises the stakes just enough to matter.
- Create a "Wash" Drill: In a wash drill, a team has to win two or three points in a row to score a single point. This teaches teams how to string together good plays and handle the pressure of a "must-win" point.

Integrated Conditioning: The End of "Running for Punishment"

The old way of conditioning was to run lines or sprints at the end of practice. The new, more effective way is to integrate conditioning directly into your volleyball drills. Why? Because it's more specific to the game. Players don't just run in a straight line in volleyball; they shuffle, they jump, they dive, and they do it all while trying to play the ball. Integrated conditioning trains their bodies and minds at the same time.

How to Integrate Conditioning

- Increase the Pace: Give players less time between reps. This forces them to work harder and simulates the cardiovascular demands of a long rally.

- Add a Movement: Before a player can perform a skill, make them do a movement. For example, before a player can hit, they have to touch the 10-foot line and then transition to attack. This adds a conditioning element to every hitting drill.
- Use Multi-Ball Drills: Instead of one ball, have a coach initiate a second or third ball immediately after the first one. This keeps the drill moving and forces players to work continuously.

Example: The "Never-Ending Sixes" Drill

This is a classic, high-energy 6v6 drill that is great for conditioning. One team starts with a free ball. The rally is played out. As soon as the rally ends, a coach immediately sends a second free ball to the other team. The drill continues for a set period (e.g., 5 minutes). It's chaotic, it's tiring, and it's one of the most game-like ways to train your team to play hard when they are fatigued.

Reading the Room: The Art of Adjusting on the Fly

No practice plan is perfect. A great coach knows how to read the energy of the gym and adjust on the fly. Is the energy low? Maybe it's time for a fun, competitive game. Are players getting frustrated with a drill? Maybe it's time to turn the dial down to the Teaching Zone and clarify the objective. Are they executing a drill perfectly? Maybe it's time to turn the dial up and add a competitive element.

Don't be a slave to your practice plan. Be a student of your team. Watch them. Listen to them. And be willing to adjust. That is the art of running a truly great practice.

FIFTEEN

Troubleshooting Common Problems

No matter how well you plan, every coach runs into the same, predictable problems. Your team is struggling with serving errors. The gym is dead quiet. Players are watching balls drop without moving their feet. It's a normal part of the coaching journey. The difference between a good coach and a great coach is not in avoiding these problems, but in knowing how to solve them.

This chapter is your troubleshooting guide. It's a collection of the most common problems you'll face and a toolbox of simple, practical solutions to fix them. For each problem, we'll look at the likely cause and a specific, actionable solution you can implement in your very next practice.

Your Troubleshooting Framework: Diagnose Before You Prescribe

When you see a problem, your first instinct will be to jump in and fix it. But before you prescribe a solution, take a moment to diagnose the root cause. A team that is making a lot of passing errors might not have a passing problem; they might have a footwork problem. A team that is quiet might not have a communication problem; they might have a confidence problem. Always ask yourself: "What's the real problem here?"

Here is a guide to some of the most common problems and how to solve them.

The Problem	The Likely Cause	The Solution
Too Many Serving Errors	Your players are either not focused or are afraid of making a mistake. They are aiming for the perfect serve instead of a good, tough serve.	The Fix: The "3-Point" Serving Game. Turn serving into a competitive game. Give players 10 serves. They get +1 point for an ace, 0 points for a serve that goes in, and -2 points for a missed serve. This scoring system rewards aggressive, smart serving and penalizes errors. It teaches them to find the balance between being tough and being consistent.
Poor Communication (A Quiet Gym)	Your players are either not confident enough to speak up or they don't know what to say. You haven't made communication a clear, non-negotiable standard.	The Fix: The "One-Word" Focus. Dedicate a practice to communication. Your one-word focus for the day is "LOUD." Praise every instance of loud communication, no matter how small. In every drill, require players to call the ball with their name. If they don't, the point is replayed. This makes it clear that communication is just as important as any physical skill.
Lack of Hustle (Balls Dropping)	Players are either physically tired or they have developed the habit of assuming their teammate will get the ball. There is no clear standard for what "hustle" looks like.	The Fix: The "Perfect 10" Drill. This is a simple drill that makes hustle a measurable standard. A coach tosses 10 balls into an empty court, in challenging but gettable spots. The six players on the court must keep every single ball from hitting the floor. If a ball drops, the drill resets to 0. This drill creates a clear, shared goal and teaches players to take responsibility for every ball.
Inconsistent Passing	The root cause of inconsistent passing is almost always poor footwork. Players are reaching for the ball with their arms instead of moving their feet to get their body behind the ball.	The Fix: The "Beat the Ball" Drill. In your passing drills, shift the focus from the platform to the feet. Use the cue: "Beat the ball to the spot." Before you toss the ball, call out a player's name. That player must move to the spot where the ball will be passed before the toss. This forces them to prioritize their footwork and creates the habit of moving first.
Players Are Making the Same Mistake Repeatedly	You are either over-coaching (giving too much feedback) or your feedback is not sticking. The players are not internalizing the correction.	The Fix: The "Question, Not Command" Method. Instead of telling them what to do, ask them a question. Instead of "You need to get your hand over the ball," ask, "What did you feel on that contact?" This forces the player to think for themselves and internalize the feeling of the correct movement. It's slower in the moment, but the learning lasts longer.
Your Team Plays Scared or Tentative	You have likely created an environment where players are afraid to make mistakes. You may be focusing too much on outcomes (winning) instead of process (playing the right way).	The Fix: The "Mistake Ritual." Create a simple, positive ritual for what to do after a mistake. It could be a player tapping their head and saying, "My bad," and their teammates responding with, "You got the next one." This normalizes mistakes, makes it clear that they are a part of the learning process, and gives players a clear, physical way to move on to the next play.

The Ultimate Troubleshooting Tool: The Video Camera

Your smartphone is one of the most powerful coaching tools you have. Players often don't believe what you are telling them until they see it with their own eyes. A short, 10-second video clip can be more effective than a 10-minute speech.

- Show, Don't Just Tell: If a player is struggling with their hitting approach, take a quick video. Show them the difference between their approach and a video of a high-level player. They will often see the problem immediately.
- Highlight the Positive: Video is not just for correcting mistakes. Catch your players doing something right. Show a video of the team executing a perfect three-pass-set-hit sequence. This is a powerful way to build confidence and reinforce what you want to see more of.

Coaching is a continuous cycle of problem-solving. Don't get discouraged when these problems pop up. See them as opportunities. They are signposts telling you exactly what your team needs to work on next. Embrace the challenge, stay curious, and keep your toolbox of solutions ready.

SIXTEEN

Parent Communication Mastery

For many new coaches, the most intimidating part of the job has nothing to do with what happens on the court. It's the parents. Managing the expectations, emotions, and questions of a dozen different families can feel like a second full-time job. But it doesn't have to be a source of stress. With a proactive system and a calm, professional approach, you can turn your parent group from a potential liability into your team's greatest asset.

This chapter is your complete guide to mastering parent communication. We'll cover how to set up a system for proactive updates, a simple framework for resolving conflicts, and how to handle those tricky situations with confidence and class.

The Golden Rule of Parent Communication: No Surprises

Almost every parent-coach conflict stems from one thing: a breakdown in communication that leads to a surprise. A player is surprised they're not playing the position they thought they were. A parent is surprised their child isn't getting more playing time. A family is surprised by a last-minute change to the tournament schedule. The single most effective thing you can do to build a positive relationship with your parents is to eliminate surprises through proactive, consistent communication.

Your Proactive Communication System: The Three "Must-Haves"

Don't wait for parents to come to you with questions. Get ahead of them with a simple, predictable communication system. This system should have three key components.

1. The Pre-Season Parent Meeting: Before your first tournament, hold a mandatory meeting for all parents. This is your chance to set the tone and establish your expectations for the season. In this meeting, you should cover:

- Your Coaching Philosophy: Share your "North Star" objective. Let them know that your primary goal is to develop their child as a player and a person.
- Your Expectations for Players: Cover your standards for effort, communication, and being a good teammate.

- Your Expectations for Parents: Ask them to be a source of positive encouragement, to cheer for the whole team, and to honor the 24-Hour Rule.
- Your Communication Plan: Explain how and when you will be communicating with them throughout the season.

2. The Weekly Update Email: Every Sunday evening, send a short, simple email to all the parents. This email should include:

- A brief recap of the previous week's practices or tournaments.
- The schedule for the upcoming week.
- One or two things the team will be focusing on in practice. This simple act of consistency builds trust and makes parents feel like they are part of the team.

3. The 24-Hour Rule: This is the most important boundary you will set. The 24-Hour Rule states that you will not discuss playing time, strategy, or any other emotionally charged topic with a parent within 24 hours of a match. This allows for a cooling-off period and ensures that any conversation you have is productive, not emotional. Introduce this rule at your pre-season meeting and stick to it.

The Art of Conflict Resolution: The "Listen, Acknowledge, Explain" Framework

Even with a great communication system, conflicts will still arise. A parent will be upset about their child's playing time. A player will be frustrated with their role on the team. How you handle these moments will define your leadership. When faced with a conflict, use this simple, three-step framework.

Step	What It Is	What It Sounds Like
1. Listen	Your first job is to listen. Let the parent or player say everything they need to say without interrupting. Make eye contact. Nod your head. Show them that you are hearing them.	"Thank you for coming to me with this. I want to understand. Tell me more about what you're seeing."
2. Acknowledge	After they have finished, acknowledge their feelings. You don't have to agree with them, but you do have to validate their emotion. This de-escalates the situation and shows that you respect their perspective.	"I can hear how frustrating this is for you. It makes sense that you're upset. I would be, too, if I saw it that way."
3. Explain (Your "Why")	Now, and only now, do you explain your decision. Don't be defensive. Simply and calmly explain the "why" behind your coaching decision, connecting it back to the team's goals and your coaching philosophy.	"The reason Sarah is playing in the back row right now is because her serve receive has become one of the most consistent on the team, and we need that stability to run our offense. We are still working on her blocking footwork in practice, and as soon as that becomes more consistent, she will have an opportunity to play more in the front row."

Handling Tricky Situations: Your Prepared Responses

There are a few tricky situations that every coach will face. Having a prepared, professional response in your back pocket will help you handle them with grace.

- The Sideline Coach: The parent who is coaching their child from the stands. Your Response: At a break in the action, calmly walk over to the parent and say, "I know you're just trying to help, but in order for the team to be successful, they need to be focused on one voice right now. I would really appreciate it if you could let me do the coaching, and you can focus on being a positive, supportive fan."
- The Post-Game Ambush: The parent who corners you right after a tough loss to complain about playing time. Your Response: "I really appreciate you wanting to talk about this, and I want to hear what you have to say. But the 24-Hour Rule is really important for making sure we have a productive conversation. Can you send me an email tomorrow, and we can set up a time to chat?"
- The "My Child is the Best" Parent: The parent who believes their child is the star and should never come off the court. Your Response: Use the Listen, Acknowledge, Explain framework. Listen to their perspective. Acknowledge their

passion. Then, explain your decisions in the context of what is best for the entire team.

Parent communication is not about being perfect. It's about being professional, proactive, and patient. If you treat your players' parents with respect, communicate with them consistently, and always keep the focus on what's best for the team, you will build a powerful and positive partnership that will last the entire season.

PART V
End-of-Season Excellence

SEVENTEEN

Preparing for Finals & Big Events

You've made it. After months of hard work, your team has earned the right to compete in the most important matches of the year. The end of the season is not the time for new skills or complex strategies. It's the time for clarity, confidence, and a relentless focus on what you do best. Your job as the coach is to get out of the way, simplify everything, and create an environment where your players can walk onto the court for their biggest match feeling calm, confident, and prepared to execute.

This chapter is your guide to peaking at the right time. We'll cover the mindset shift required for championship season, the art of simplifying your strategy, and how to fine-tune your team's execution so they are sharp when it matters most.

The Championship Mindset: Simplify to Amplify

The biggest mistake coaches make at the end of the season is trying to do too much. They add new plays, overanalyze opponents, and cram their practice plans with a dozen different drills. This doesn't build confidence; it creates confusion and anxiety. The key to a championship season is to simplify to amplify. You are not going to teach your players a new skill in the week before the final. But you can amplify their confidence, their execution, and their belief in each other by simplifying your message and your focus. Your mantra for the end of the season should be: "Do what you do, but do it better than you ever have before."

Sharpen Your Sword: Double Down on Your Strengths

Now is not the time to worry about your weaknesses. It's the time to sharpen your sword—to identify the one or two things your team does best and dedicate the majority of your practice time to making them unstoppable. Are you a great serving team? Spend half of your practice on competitive serving games. Are you a scrappy defensive team? Spend your time in long, chaotic, game-like rallies. By focusing on your strengths, you build a clear, confident identity that your team can rely on under pressure.

The 80/20 Rule of Scouting

Scouting your opponent is important, but it can also be a trap. It's easy to get so caught up in what the other team does that you forget about what you do. A simple way to avoid this is to use the 80/20 Rule.

- 80% of your focus should be on your side of the net. Your execution, your communication, your energy.
- 20% of your focus should be on the opponent. Identify one or two key tendencies of your opponent and give your team a simple, actionable game plan. Don't give them a 10-page scouting report. Give them one or two things to look for.

Opponent Tendency	Your Simple Game Plan
Their star hitter always hits the line.	"When she's in the front row, our line blocker is taking away the line, and our defender is starting in the cross-court."
They have a weak server.	"When she is serving, we are running our fastest, most aggressive offense. This is our chance to score."

Simple, clear, and actionable. That's the key to a good scouting report.

Your Pre-Finals Practice Plan: Short, Sharp, and Game-Like

The week before a big event, your practices should get shorter, sharper, and more intense. The goal is not to wear your players out; it's to get them mentally and physically sharp. Here's what a pre-finals practice should look like:

- Shorter Duration: A 75-minute practice is better than a 2-hour practice the week of a final. You want your players to leave the gym feeling fresh and confident, not exhausted.
- Game-Like Drills Only: No more standing in lines. Every drill should be a 6v6, competitive, game-like situation. Keep score in everything. Make it feel like a real match.
- High-Intensity, Low-Volume: The pace of practice should be fast, with quick transitions between drills. But you should be doing fewer reps overall. Quality over quantity.

- End on a High Note: The last drill of your last practice before the final should be a fun, competitive game that your team loves to play. You want them to walk out of the gym with a smile on their face, feeling good about themselves and their teammates.

The Final Message: Trust Your Training

Your last team meeting before the big match should be your shortest one of the season. Your players don't need a long, emotional speech. They need a calm, confident leader who believes in them. Your message should be simple:

"Everything we need to be successful, we have already built. We have put in the work. We have faced challenges and grown together. We are prepared. Today is not about doing anything special. It's about trusting our training, trusting each other, and playing with the joy and confidence that got us here. Go have fun. I'm proud of you."

And then, you let them go. You've done your job. Now it's time to let them do theirs.

EIGHTEEN

End-of-Year Success: What Really Matters

The final whistle has blown. The season is over. The gym is quiet. Whether your last game ended in a championship trophy or a heartbreaking loss, the question every coach asks themselves is the same: "Was it a successful season?"

It's easy to define success by the number in the "win" column. But that's a shallow and fleeting measure. The true impact of your coaching, the success that lasts a lifetime, is measured in something far more profound: the growth of the young people you were privileged to lead.

This chapter is your guide to measuring what really matters. We'll explore the three true pillars of a successful season: player growth, team culture, and your own development as a coach. This is how you measure your true impact.

The Real Scoreboard: Measuring Player Growth

Forget the win-loss record for a moment. The real scoreboard is the progress your players made from the first day of tryouts to the last day of the season. This is the heart of developmental coaching. At the end of the year, ask yourself these questions about each of your players:

- Did they improve as a volleyball player? Did their serve get more consistent? Did their passing get more accurate? Did they finally master that footwork pattern you worked on all season? Celebrate the small, individual victories. That is the mark of real coaching.
- Did they grow as a person? Did the shy player start to communicate more on the court? Did the star player learn how to be a better teammate? Did the player who was always hard on herself learn how to handle mistakes with more grace? This is the growth that matters most.
- Did they have a positive experience? In ten years, your players will not remember the score of a single match. But they will remember how you made them feel. Did they feel seen, supported, and valued? Did they have fun? Did they fall more in love with the game? That is the ultimate measure of a successful season.

The Legacy You Leave: Your Team Culture

Your team culture is the legacy you leave behind. It's the set of standards, values, and behaviors that will endure long after the season is over. It's what your players will take with them to their next team, their next classroom, and their next job. When you look back on your season, ask yourself:

- Did we build a culture of resilience? When things got tough, did your team come together or fall apart? Did they learn how to handle adversity with courage and grace?
- Did we build a culture of support? How did your players treat each other? Did they celebrate each other's successes? Did they pick each other up after a mistake? The quality of your team's relationships is a direct reflection of your leadership.
- Did we build a culture of effort? Did your players learn the value of hard work? Did they take pride in giving their best effort, regardless of the outcome? A team that hustles is a team that has learned one of the most important lessons in sports and in life.

The Lasting Impact

In the end, the trophies gather dust. The banners fade. But the impact you have on a young person's life is permanent. If you have helped your players grow as athletes and as people, if you have built a culture of resilience and support, then you have had a profoundly successful season, no matter what the final scoreboard said. And that is something to be truly proud of.

Final Reflections & Coach Growth

The end of the season is not just a time for your players to reflect; it's a critical moment in your own journey as a coach. The lessons you learn from your first season—the successes, the failures, the moments of frustration, and the moments of pure joy—are the raw material for your growth. The best coaches are not the ones who know everything; they are the ones who are the most curious, the most reflective, and the most committed to their own development. Your journey as a coach is just beginning.

The Coach's Post-Season Review: A Framework for Growth

Just as you asked your players to reflect on their growth, you must do the same for yourself. In the quiet week after the season ends, before you get swept up in the next thing, take an hour for yourself. Grab a notebook and use this simple, three-part framework to guide your reflection.

1. The "Keep, Stop, Start" Method: This is a powerful and simple tool for honest self-assessment.

- What is one thing I did this season that I want to keep doing? (Maybe it was your weekly update email to parents, or the way you structured your practices.)
- What is one thing I did this season that I need to stop doing? (Maybe you were too negative during games, or you didn't delegate enough.)
- What is one thing I want to start doing next season? (Maybe you want to start using video more, or you want to do individual player check-ins.)

2. Revisit Your Philosophy: Pull out that coaching philosophy you wrote at the beginning of the season. Read it again. Ask yourself: "Did I live up to this? Where did I succeed, and where did I fall short?" This is not an exercise in self-criticism. It's an exercise in self-awareness. Your philosophy is not a static document; it's a living, breathing guide that you should revisit and refine every single year.

3. Identify Your Biggest "Growth Moment": Think back on the entire season. What was the single most challenging moment for you as a coach? Maybe it was a conflict with a parent, a tough loss, or a player who was struggling. How did you handle it? What did you learn from it? Your biggest challenges are always your greatest teachers.

The Art of Learning from Your Mistakes: Your "Mistake Resume"

Every coach makes mistakes. It's part of the job. The difference between a good coach and a great coach is not that they don't make mistakes; it's that they learn from them. One of the most powerful exercises you can do is to create a "mistake resume."

At the end of each season, write down the 2-3 biggest mistakes you made. For each mistake, write down:

- The Mistake: (e.g., "I was too focused on winning and lost sight of player development.")
- The Impact: (e.g., "The players felt a lot of pressure, and some of them lost their love for the game.")
- The Lesson: (e.g., "Next season, I will define success by player growth, not just the scoreboard.")

This is not about beating yourself up. It's about taking ownership of your growth. Your mistake resume will become one of your most valuable coaching documents, a powerful reminder of the lessons you've learned on your journey.

Developing Your Identity: The Never-Ending Journey

Your coaching identity is not something you find; it's something you build, season by season, mistake by mistake, reflection by reflection. It is the sum of your philosophy, your experiences, and your commitment to growth. The journey to becoming the coach you want to be is a marathon, not a sprint. Here are a few ways to stay on the path.

- Find a Mentor: Find a more experienced coach who you admire and ask if you can buy them a cup of coffee. Ask them about their journey, their mistakes, and their biggest lessons. You don't have to do this alone.
- Be a Student of the Game (and of People): Watch more volleyball. Read books about leadership and psychology. Listen to podcasts. The best coaches are always learning, not just about the X's and O's, but about how to connect with and motivate people.
- Remember Your "Why": On the tough days, and there will be tough days, always come back to your "why." Why did you start coaching in the first place? For the love of the game? For the opportunity to make a positive impact on young people's lives? Your "why" is your anchor. It will keep you grounded and focused on what truly matters.

The Coach's Promise

Your first season is in the books. You made it. You have learned more than you ever thought possible, not just about volleyball, but about leadership, about people, and about yourself. The journey of a coach is one of the most challenging and rewarding paths you can take. Embrace the process. Stay curious. Be kind to yourself. And never forget the profound impact you have the privilege of making in the lives of your players. The best is yet to come.

NINETEEN

Looking Ahead to Year Two

Your first season is a whirlwind of learning, adapting, and surviving. Your second season is where you begin to build. You have a foundation of experience to stand on, a clearer understanding of your own coaching identity, and a wealth of lessons learned from your mistakes. Year two is your opportunity to move from reactive to proactive, from surviving to thriving. It's your chance to take everything you've learned and begin building a program with long-term stability and a culture of excellence.

This final chapter is your guide to making the leap from year one to year two. We'll cover how to intentionally improve as a coach, how to create systems to stay organized, how to upgrade your drill library, and how to start thinking like a program builder, not just a single-season coach.

From Experience to Expertise: The 1% Rule

The secret to long-term growth as a coach is not to try to reinvent yourself every year; it's to get 1% better in a few key areas. Based on your post-season reflection, pick one or two specific, manageable things you want to improve on in your second season. Maybe it's your parent communication. Maybe it's your in-game decision-making. Maybe it's your ability to teach a specific skill. Don't try to fix everything. Focus on small, incremental improvements. That is the path to mastery.

Building Your "Second Brain": Systems for Staying Organized

In your first year, you were probably scrambling to keep everything straight. In your second year, you can build systems to do the heavy lifting for you. Think of this as building your coaching "second brain"—a set of simple, repeatable systems that will save you time, reduce your stress, and allow you to focus on what really matters: coaching your players.

- Your Drill Library: Don't just save your drills; organize them. Create a simple folder on your computer with subfolders for each skill (e.g., "Serving Drills," "Passing Drills," "Competitive 6v6 Games"). Check the last section of the book for

additional drills to expand your library. After each practice, take 5 minutes to jot down a few notes on the drills you ran. Did they work? What would you change next time?
- Your Practice Plan Template: Create a simple, reusable template for your practice plans. This will save you hours over the course of a season. Your template should include your 5-part practice structure we discussed in Chapter 9, and you can simply fill in the specific drills for each day.
- Your Communication Templates: Save your weekly update email and your pre-season parent meeting agenda as templates. This will make your communication more consistent and less time-consuming.

Upgrading Your Drills: The Art of the "Plus One"

Now that you have a season of experience, you can start to upgrade your drills. A simple way to do this is with the "Plus One" method. Take a drill that you ran last season and add one small element to make it more game-like, more competitive, or more challenging.

Your Year One Drill	The "Plus One" Upgrade for Year Two
A simple passing drill where you toss balls to your players.	Plus One: The coach now serves the ball, forcing the players to read a real serve.
A 6v6 scrimmage where you just play.	Plus One: You add a "wash" scoring system, where a team has to win two points in a row to score one point.
A hitting drill where players hit lines.	Plus One: You add a real block, forcing the hitters to learn to hit around a defender.

Small, simple upgrades like these will keep your practices fresh and will continually challenge your players to grow.

Building for the Long-Term: The Program-Builder's Mindset

In your second year, you can start to think beyond just this season. You can start thinking like a program builder. This means making decisions that will not only help your current team but will also lay the foundation for the long-term health and stability of your program.

- Develop Your Younger Players: Don't just focus on your starters. Invest time and energy in your younger players and your bench. Their development is the future of your program.
- Create a Leadership Pipeline: Identify potential leaders on your team and give them opportunities to grow. Maybe you create a "leadership council," or you give your older players mentoring roles with the younger players.
- Build Relationships with Your Feeder Program: Get to know the coaches at the middle school or the club that feeds into your program. Share your philosophy. Offer to run a clinic. Building these relationships will create a more consistent and positive experience for players as they move up.

Your Journey Continues

Congratulations, coach. You have navigated the challenges of your first season and are ready to take the next step on your journey. The path of a coach is a never-ending process of learning, reflecting, and growing. Embrace the journey. Stay curious. And never forget the profound and lasting impact you have the privilege of making.

Welcome to year two. You've got this.

PART VI
The 25 Core Drills Every Coach Needs

This section is organized to help players, coaches, and teams progress through every phase of the game—from controlled fundamentals to dynamic team systems.

Each drill builds upon the previous one, strengthening both individual technique and team cohesion.

You'll notice that the drills are grouped around major volleyball roles and skill areas:

- Serving and Pressure Training: Develop consistency, accuracy, and composure under game-like tension.
- Ball Control and Passing: Improve first-contact quality and rhythm between players.
- Setting and Blocking: Build technical precision and timing for front-row players.
- Coverage and Transition: Strengthen teamwork, defensive recovery, and offensive execution.

Each position on the court demands a unique combination of technical precision, speed, and game awareness.

Use the following summary to focus training based on the player's position:

- **Setters**
  - Core Focus: Setting accuracy, timing, transition awareness.
  - Recommended Drills: 3, 10, 13, 16, 21, 22.

- **Liberos / Defensive Specialists**
  - Core Focus: Serve-receive, reaction, coverage control.
  - Recommended Drills: 2, 4, 7, 9, 11, 12, 14, 15, 17, 18, 23, 25.

- **Hitters / Middles**
  - Core Focus: Block timing, attacking power, first-ball side-outs.
  - Recommended Drills: 6, 8, 14, 16, 18, 20, 22, 24, 25.

- **Servers / All Players**
  - Core Focus: Consistency, placement, composure under pressure.
  - Recommended Drills: 1, 5, 17, 19, 24, 25.

Tip: Rotate through all drills over time to develop a complete game foundation, even if players specialize in one position.

To get the most out of this:

1. Record performance for each drill.
2. Repeat each drill regularly, aiming to raise benchmarks week by week.
3. Rotate drills by position or training focus—setters can repeat Drill 3 weekly, liberos can prioritize Drills 2, 4, and 9, and hitters should focus on Drills 6, 7, and 10.

Every drill is designed to be flexible—adaptable for solo, partner, or team practice. Use them to build confidence, challenge consistency, and sharpen tactical thinking.

Volleyball performance connects body, mind, and teamwork. The drills in this section are sequenced to mirror real match flow—from the serve that starts play, through the pass, set, attack, and recovery. Whether working with individuals, small groups, or a full team, use this sequence to guide athletes through a complete game cycle of skill, communication, and mental focus.

Structured Play Development

Drill Index by Position

Each volleyball position requires a unique mix of skills—from the precision of a setter's hands to the fast reactions of a libero and the timing of a hitter at the net.

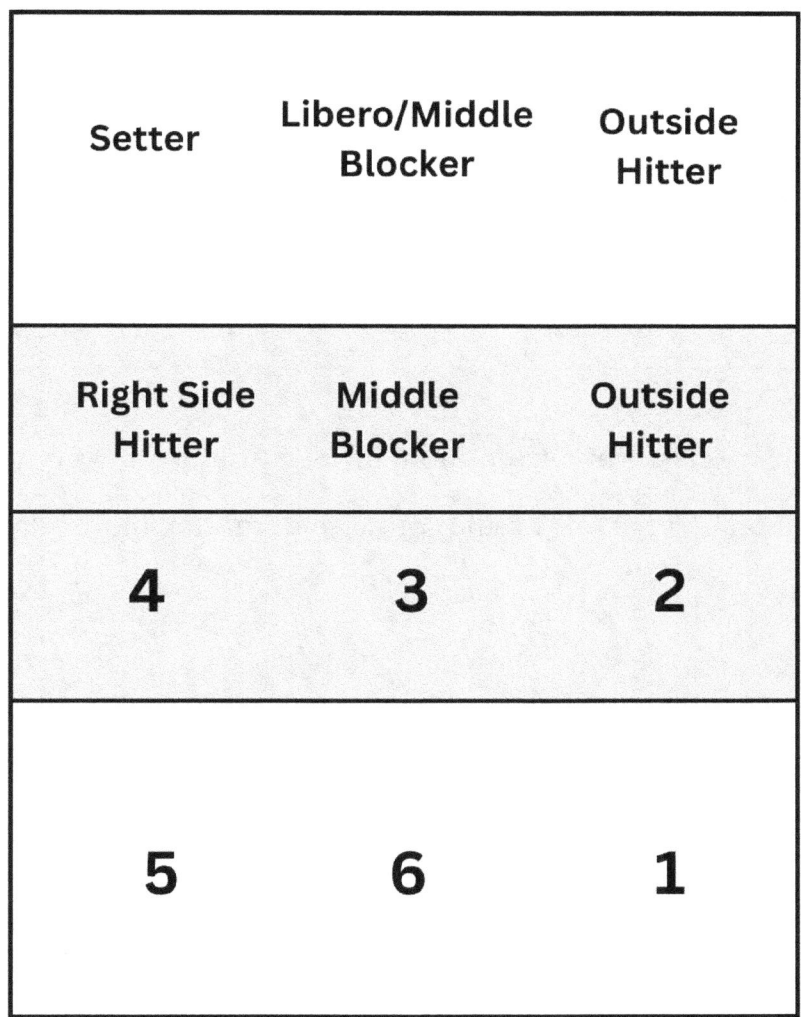

Figure A. Standard volleyball rotation layout showing base positions for each role.

Use this index to organize training around drills that match players' priorities while rotating through all drills for a complete, balanced game.

Position	Recommended Drills	Primary Focus
Setters	3, 10, 13, 16, 21, 22	Setting accuracy, timing, and transition awareness
Liberos / Defensive Specialists	2, 4, 7, 9, 11, 12, 14, 15, 17, 18, 23, 25	Serve-receive, reaction, and coverage control
Hitters / Middles	6, 8, 14, 16, 18, 20, 22, 24, 25	Block timing, attacking power, and first-ball side-outs
Servers / All Players	1, 5, 17, 19, 24, 25	Consistency, placement, and composure under pressure

Tip: Even if players specialize in one position, include drills from every category.

Coaches who understand every role on the court build smarter, more adaptable teams.

Skill Progression Overview

The drills in this section are designed to follow the natural rhythm of a volleyball match—from the serve that begins play to the pass, set, attack, and recovery.

By practicing them in order, players develop a complete foundation of technical skill, court awareness, and teamwork.

Use the chart below to understand how each stage builds upon the next:

Stage	Primary Focus	Drills	Key Skills Developed
Stage 1 – Serve Foundation	Accuracy, placement, and routine	1, 5, 17, 19, 24	Controlled serving, mental preparation, and tactical focus
Stage 2 – First Contact	Ball control and passing precision	2, 4, 7, 9, 11, 12, 15, 18, 23	Platform control, movement efficiency, and consistent passing angles
Stage 3 – Setting & Blocking	Precision and timing in front-row play	3, 6, 10, 13, 16, 22	Hand positioning, tempo control, and jump timing
Stage 4 – Team Systems	Communication and reaction	7, 14, 15, 18, 21, 25	Defensive recovery, positioning, and coordinated coverage
Stage 5 – Transition & Attack	Converting defense into offense	8, 10, 14, 16, 20, 23, 25	Quick transitions, approach timing, and attack execution

Tip: Treat each stage as a weekly or biweekly focus area. Once your players have met the benchmarks for one stage, progress to the next to simulate full match flow and balanced skill development.

Dual Measurements Reference (Feet + Meters)

Volleyball training often uses both imperial and metric measurements. Use this chart to quickly convert distances and ensure accuracy, whether you're coaching in the U.S. or abroad.

All drills in this section include both feet and meter equivalents for clarity.

Feet (ft)	Meters (m)	Common Use in Drills
3 ft	0.9 m	Jump reach or small step spacing
6 ft	1.8 m	Short pass or footwork shuffle distance
8 ft	2.4 m	Close-range net or wall drills
10 ft	3 m	Standard hitting or blocking approach distance
15 ft	4.5 m	Partner pepper or mid-range passing
20 ft	6 m	Serve target or long control drill spacing
30 ft	9 m	Full half-court serve or deep defensive range

Tip: If you coach internationally, tape these conversions on your gym wall or notebook for quick reference.

Being comfortable with both systems helps when reviewing drills or communicating with coaches and players worldwide.

Drill 1: Serving with a Purpose

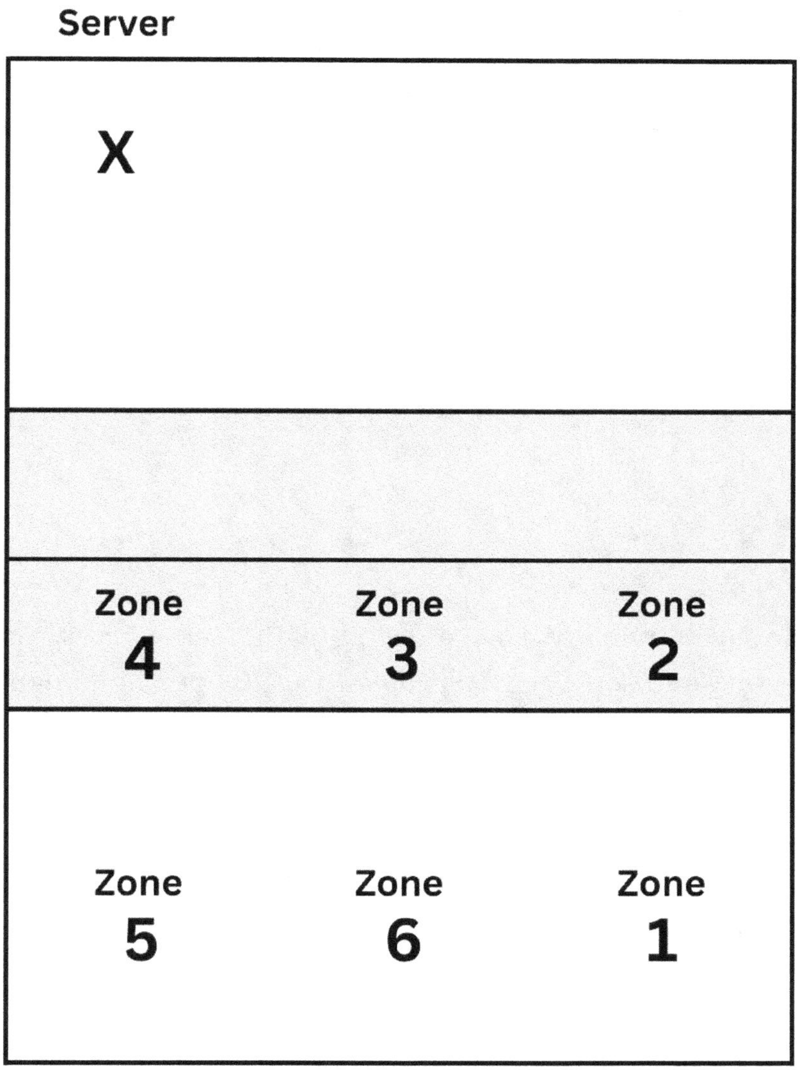

Server

X		

Zone 4	Zone 3	Zone 2
Zone 5	Zone 6	Zone 1

Figure 1. Serving to five target zones across the opponent's court for accuracy and control.

Primary Roles: Servers – All positions.

Why This Matters

Serving sets the tone for every rally. It's the one skill entirely under a player's control, yet many treat it as routine rather than a tactical skill. A precise serve can destabilize the opponent's offense, disrupt rhythm, and shift momentum immediately. This drill develops accuracy, consistency, and tactical intent behind every serve.

What You'll Need

A regulation court or gym space, a basket of volleyballs, and four to five marked target zones on the opposite side—such as short left, deep left, short right, deep right, and middle. Tape or cones work well for marking. A notebook or phone can help track performance over time.

Let's Do It

Begin with your standard serving routine: a deep breath, focused eyes, and a consistent toss. Choose one target zone and serve ten balls toward it. Record how many land successfully within the area. Move to the next zone and repeat until all zones have been targeted.

Perform two full rounds, aiming to improve accuracy in the second. Focus on a consistent toss height (just above full arm extension) and solid contact at the ball's equator for control. Between serves, reset your stance—feet shoulder-width apart, front toe pointing toward the target, weight balanced over the lead foot.

Pro Tips from the Court

A controlled toss is the foundation of every good serve. Keep your elbow high and shoulders square, and strike through the ball rather than lifting upward. Visualize the trajectory before contact. Consistency in the pre-serve routine reduces anxiety and builds trust in your form.

Take It Up a Notch

Shrink your target zones or introduce goal scoring—one point per successful serve. Challenge yourself to beat previous accuracy records. To simulate pressure, assign game scenarios (for example, "24–23 championship point") and serve as if the match depends on it.

Here's an example of how to record your serving results.

Date	Target Zone	Total Serves	Accuracy %	Notes / Adjustments
MM/DD	Zone 1	10	80%	Toss too high on 2 misses
MM/DD	Zone 5	10	70%	Focus on shoulder alignment
MM/DD	Zone 6	10	90%	Excellent consistency
MM/DD	Zone 4	10	60%	Aim higher, adjust toss forward
MM/DD	Zone 2	10	80%	Good rhythm overall

Common Mistakes & Fixes

- **Mistake:** Toss drifting forward or behind.
    - **Fix:** Practice stationary toss repetitions; the ball should peak directly above the front shoulder.
- **Mistake:** Over-swinging for power.
    - **Fix:** Focus on contact timing and follow-through rather than force.
- **Mistake:** Inconsistent stance or routine.
    - **Fix:** Repeat the identical pre-serve pattern before every rep.

Benchmarks by Level

- **Beginner:** 6 of 10 serves land within the target zone consistently.
- **Intermediate:** 8 of 10 accurate serves across three different zones.
- **Advanced:** 9 of 10 precise serves, including deep-corner and short-zone placement.

How This Connects

Precision serving transitions naturally into Drill 6 – Serving Under Pressure, where athletes apply the same mechanics under competitive pressure.

Drill 2: Passing with Consistency

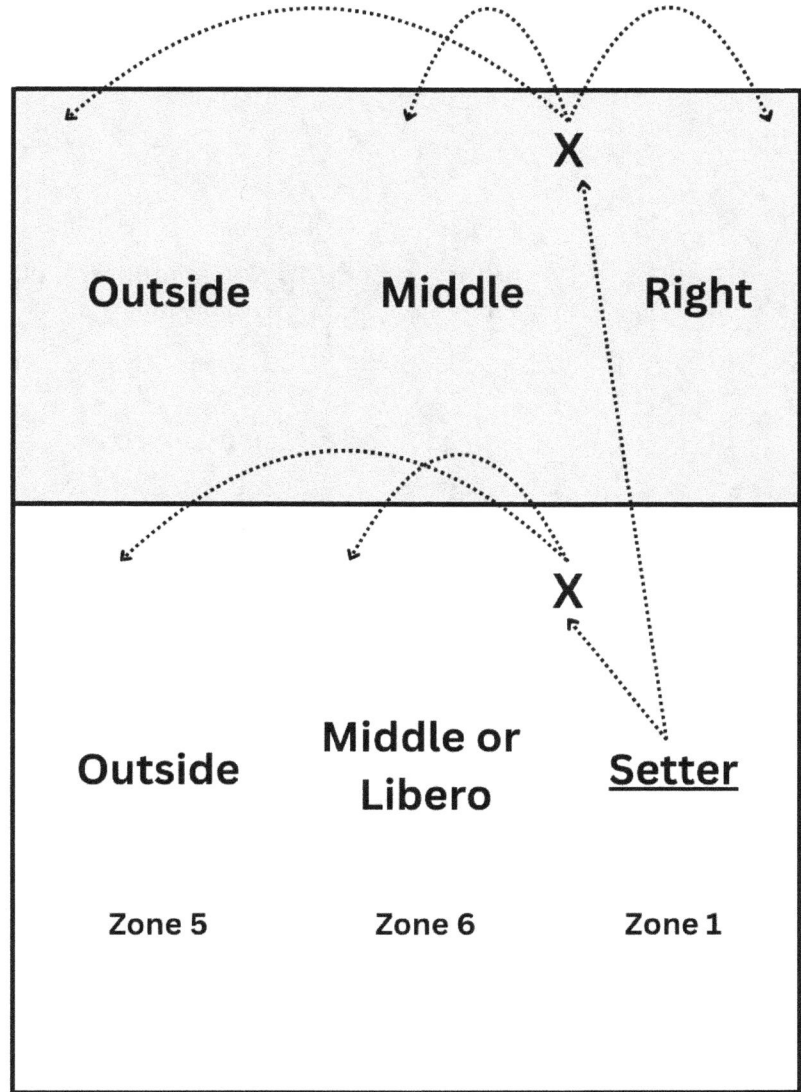

Figure 2. Three passers rotating through Zones 5, 6, and 1, passing to the setter's target area.

Primary Roles: Liberos & defensive specialists.

Why This Matters

Passing initiates offense. When the first contact is controlled, the team's entire system operates smoothly. This drill reinforces reliable posture, controlled platform angles, and quick, efficient footwork—skills essential for every position.

What You'll Need

A teammate, coach, or wall for rebounding passes; tape or a small towel to mark the target area representing the setter's zone; and 15–20 volleyballs.

Let's Do It

Begin in an athletic stance—knees bent, hips low, back flat, and arms relaxed. Have your partner serve or toss balls toward you. Pass each ball cleanly into the marked target zone using controlled platform angles. Move your feet before extending your arms; efficient movement creates consistent contact.

Complete three timed rounds, focusing on one zone at a time.

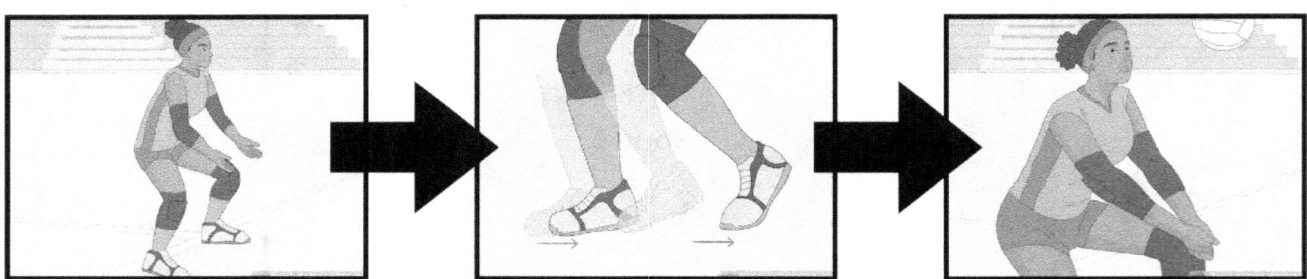

Use the following table to guide your passing sequence. Each round targets one zone at a time to promote directional control and footwork precision.

Round	Target Zone	Duration	Focus	Notes / Results
1	Zone 6 (Middle)	1 minute	Center passing control and quick foot adjustment	
2	Zone 5 (Left)	1 minute	Shuffle movement and angle correction	
3	Zone 1 (Right)	1 minute	Directional passing and shoulder alignment	

Pro Tips from the Court

Maintain quiet arms—minimal swing and firm elbows. Keep eyes level with the ball through contact. Small adjustments in platform tilt make significant changes in trajectory.

Take It Up a Notch

Add directional movement: start in zone 6, shuffle to zone 5 or 1 before passing. Vary serve speeds or trajectories. For advanced practice, alternate forearm and overhead passes to simulate broken plays.

Common Mistakes & Fixes

- **Mistake:** Reaching instead of moving.
    - **Fix:** Prioritize quick shuffles; avoid crossing feet.
- **Mistake:** Dropping elbows at contact.
    - **Fix:** Lock arms early and drive through the ball.
- **Mistake:** Leaning back on float serves.
    - **Fix:** Shift weight slightly forward—nose over toes.

Benchmarks by Level

- **Beginner:** 10 accurate passes in 3 minutes.
- **Intermediate:** 15 accurate passes with minimal directional errors.
- **Advanced:** 20 precise passes in sequence from varied serves.

How This Connects

With reliable serve-receive control in place, the next section builds offensive structure and precision through setting drills.

Mastering controlled passing prepares athletes for Drill 9 – First Ball Side-Out, where the first contact directly impacts offensive success.

Drill 3: Setting for Accuracy

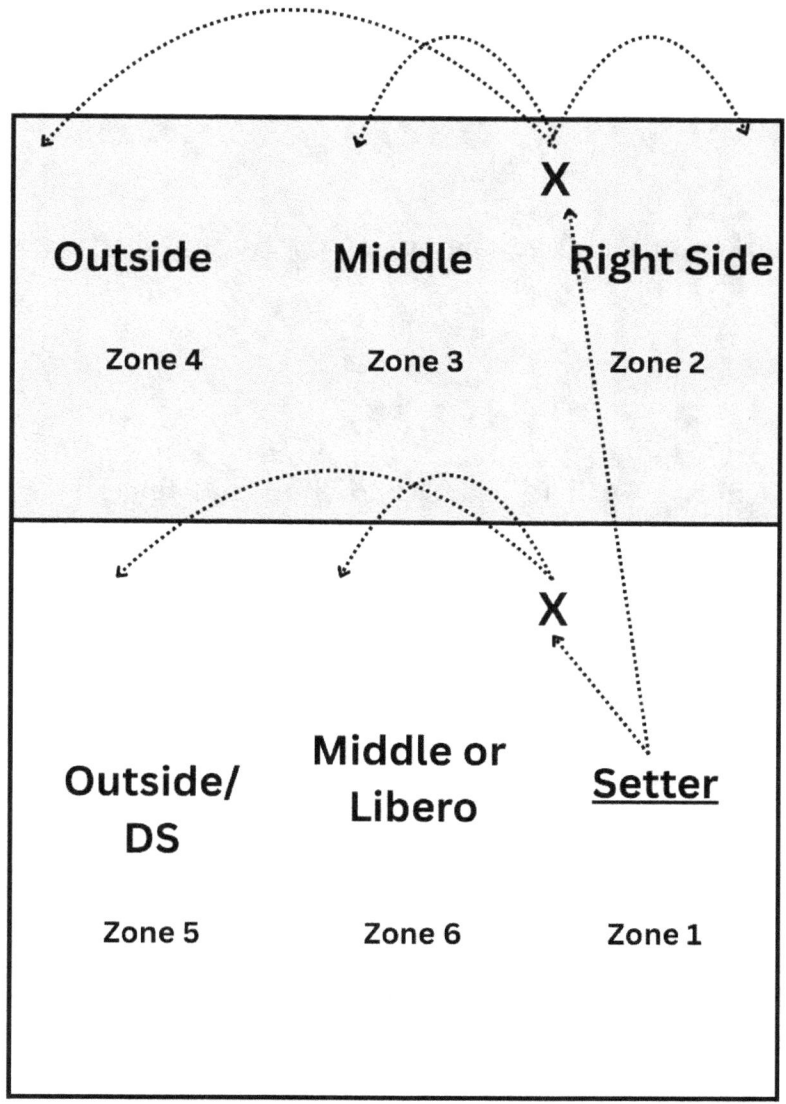

Figure 3. Setting to three attack locations—outside, middle, and back-row—from a central position.

Primary Roles: Setters – All positions.

Why This Matters

A precise set transforms potential chaos into opportunity. This drill refines hand positioning, body alignment, and tempo control to deliver hittable balls every time.

What You'll Need

One volleyball, a marked target area (cone or taped X), and 8–10 feet (2.4–3 meters) of space.

Let's Do It

Start with self-sets against a wall to establish rhythm and fingertip control. Progress to setting toward designated targets—outside, middle, and back row—cycling through each zone in three-set sequences.

Focus on soft hands, quick wrists, and square hips. Contact the ball above the forehead using fingertips, not palms. Extend fully through the wrists on release to guide the trajectory.

Pro Tips from the Court

Balance precedes precision. Keep weight evenly distributed through the balls of your feet. Avoid excessive spin by matching hand speed and pressure.

Take It Up a Notch

Add lateral movement before setting: sprint from zone 5 to 2, stop, and deliver a precise set. Introduce jump-setting once accuracy is reliable.

Common Mistakes & Fixes

- **Mistake:** Palming or catching the ball.
    - **Fix:** Emphasize fingertip control; release quickly on contact.
- **Mistake:** Off-balance sets.
    - **Fix:** Square shoulders and hips to target before release.
- **Mistake:** Over-rotation of wrists.
    - **Fix:** Keep thumbs pointed toward the forehead at setup.

Benchmarks by Level

- **Beginner:** 7 of 10 sets land in the target area.
- **Intermediate:** 8 of 10 consistent, minimal spin.
- **Advanced:** 9 of 10 accurate under movement or jump conditions.

How This Connects

Once setting rhythm and tempo are established, players can strengthen their ball control and reaction time through partner-based drills.

Accurate setting supports the transition to Drill 11 – Transition Attack, where quick offensive execution depends on precise sets after defensive plays.

Drill 4: No-Net Pepper

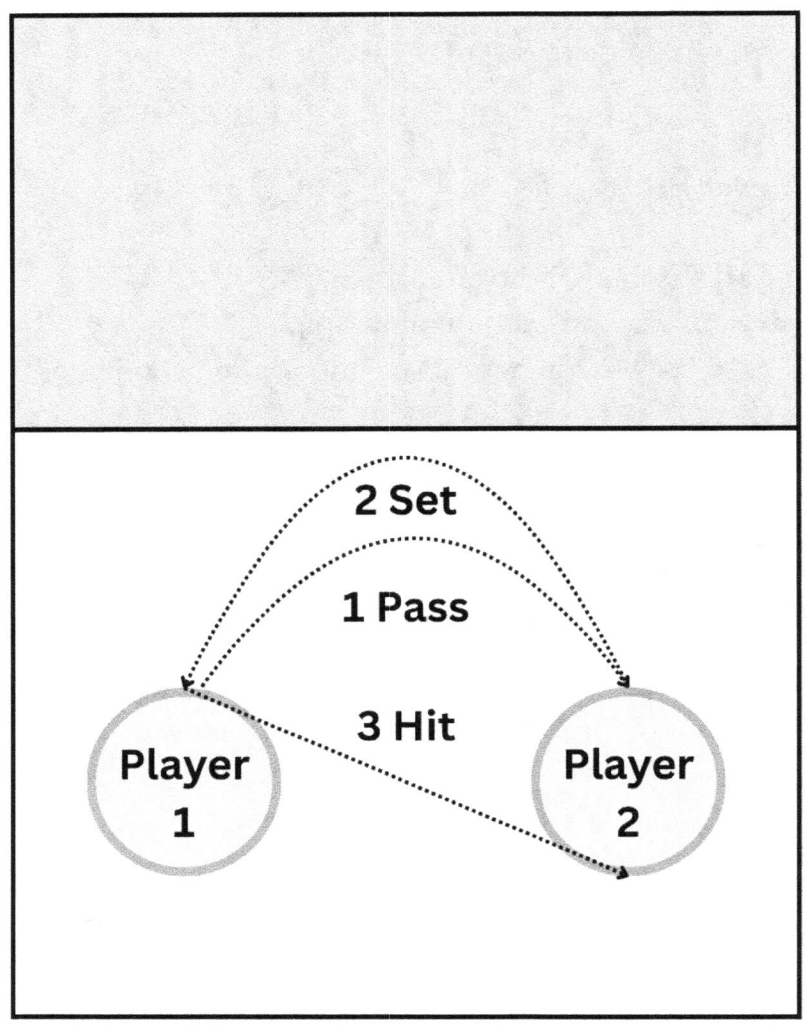

Figure 4. Partner pepper rally showing continuous pass–set–hit rhythm below net height.

Primary Roles: Liberos, defensive specialists, all players.

Why This Matters

Pepper develops control, reaction time, and rhythmic ball contact without requiring a full court. It sharpens reading and responding skills fundamental to teamwork. This drill is especially valuable for middle blockers and front-row defenders, helping them refine timing, vertical control, and coordination with the back row.

What You'll Need

One volleyball, one partner, and 10–15 feet (3–4.5 meters) of space.

Let's Do It

Players rally continuously in a pass-set-hit sequence kept below net height. Emphasize smooth transitions and clean contact rather than power. Aim for extended rallies—consistency over force.

Solo players can alternate passing and setting to a wall, focusing on ball trajectory and tempo control.

Pro Tips from the Court

Keep your knees bent and move on the balls of your feet. Engage core muscles to stabilize movement. Communicate with simple cues like "mine" or "switch" to reinforce teamwork habits.

Take It Up a Notch

Add movement patterns such as two-step shuffles between touches, or limit to one-touch pepper for speed. Alternate dominant and non-dominant contacts to enhance adaptability.

Common Mistakes & Fixes

- **Mistake:** Standing flat-footed.
    - **Fix:** Stay light and dynamic; small hops reset balance.
- **Mistake:** Over-swinging on hits.
    - **Fix:** Focus on controlled roll shots instead of spikes.

Benchmarks by Level

- **Beginner:** 20 continuous touches without error.
- **Intermediate:** 50 touches or 60 seconds uninterrupted.
- **Advanced:** 100 touches with added movement patterns.

How This Connects

After refining ball touch and coordination, it's time to apply accuracy and composure under real serving pressure.

Improved control and communication from pepper translate directly into defensive readiness for Drill 7 – Block Jump Timing and team synergy in Drill 8 – Coverage Chaos.

Drill 5: Communication Triangle Drill

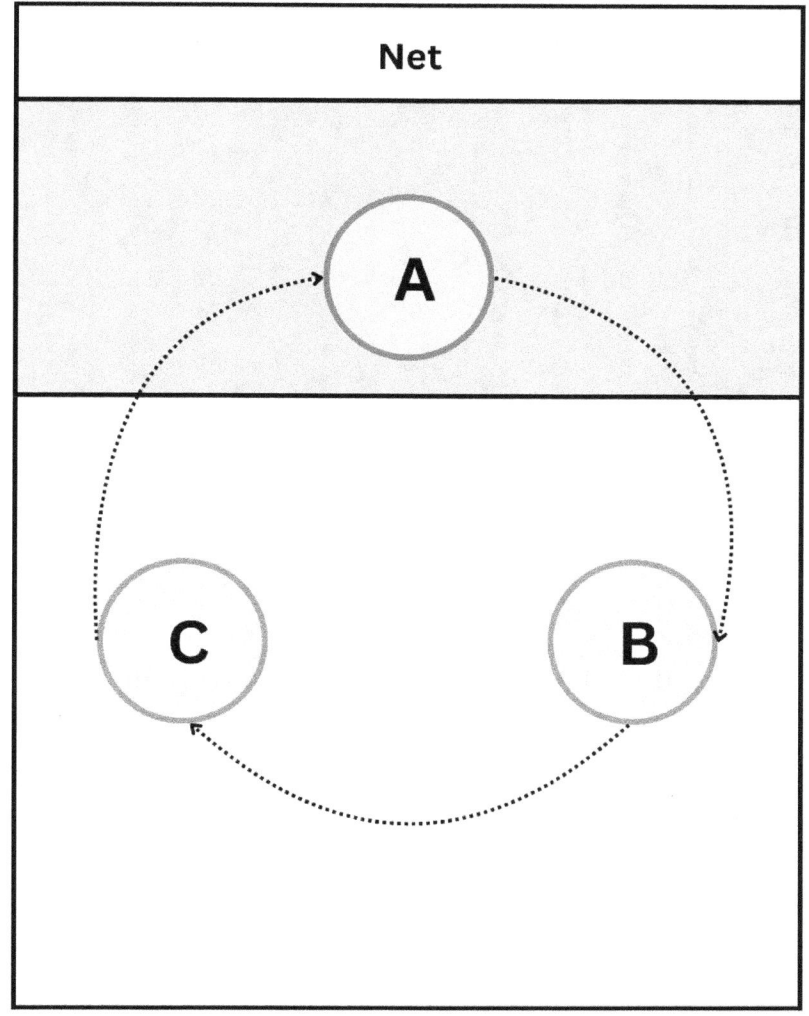

Figure 5. Communication Triangle showing three-player rotation and passing paths.

Primary Roles: All players.

Why This Matters

Communication creates rhythm. Clear, decisive calls reduce hesitation, improve ball control, and strengthen trust between teammates. This drill trains athletes to maintain constant verbal cues under movement, pressure, and rapid-fire touches—reinforcing habits that directly translate into cleaner rallies.

What You'll Need

- 3–4 players.
- One volleyball.
- Marked triangle on the court (10–12 ft / 3–3.6 m sides).
- Timer or whistle.

Let's Do It

1. Form a triangle with three players, each standing at one point.
2. Player A sends the ball to Player B; Player B must call "mine" early, receive, and pass to Player C.
3. After each pass, the passer rotates to the next cone, keeping all players in constant motion.
4. Continue for 60 seconds, counting clean contacts.
5. After each round, increase tempo or shrink spacing to increase difficulty.

Pro Tips from the Court

- Use loud, early calls: "mine," "here," "up."
- Keep the shoulders square to the next receiver.
- Prioritize height and control over power.
- Maintain eye contact before sending the ball.

Take It Up a Notch

- Add a fourth player in the middle who redirects every pass.
- Use two balls for advanced groups (requires elite communication).
- Reduce triangle size to 8 ft (2.4 m) for high-speed reps.

Common Mistakes & Fixes

- **Mistake:** Late or soft communication.
  - **Fix:** Require calls before the ball reaches peak height.
- **Mistake:** Passers drifting out of formation.
  - **Fix:** Mark rotation paths with tape.
- **Mistake:** Flat passes.
  - **Fix:** Emphasize lift from legs and core.

Benchmarks by Level

- **Beginner:** 20 clean contacts in 60 seconds.
- **Intermediate:** 35 clean contacts with full rotation.
- **Advanced:** 45+ contacts using two balls.

How This Connects

This drill sharpens the communication needed for Drill 21 – Advanced Read-Based Blocking, where verbal cues improve timing and coordination along the net.

Coach's Note

Quiet teams lose points. Loud teams win long rallies. Let your voice lead your movement.

Drill 6: Serving Under Pressure

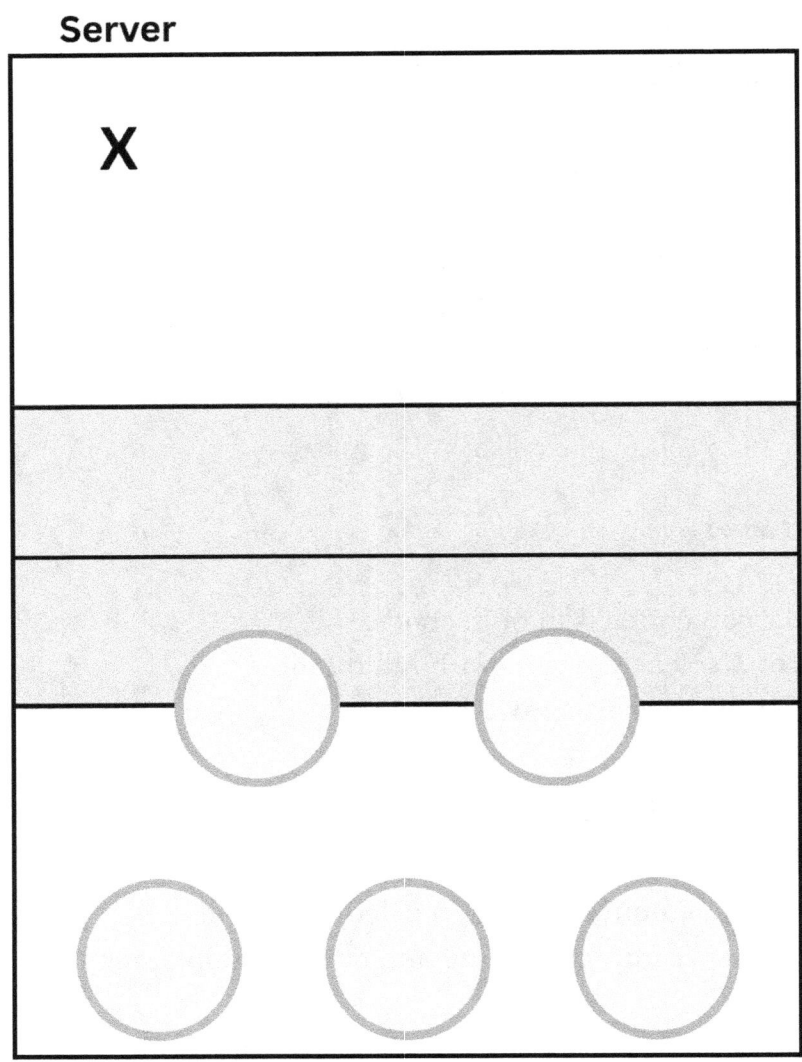

Figure 6. Pressure-serving drill using designated target zones under simulated game scenarios.

Primary Roles: Servers – All positions.

Why This Matters

Serving in practice differs from serving when the game is on the line. This drill builds mental resilience and consistency by simulating competitive stress.

What You'll Need

A volleyball court, a basket of balls, clear target zones, and a way to track score or scenario (phone, notebook, or scoreboard).

Let's Do It

Select a pressure scenario—tied 24–24, trailing 22–24, or serving after an opponent's run. Visualize the setting, take a breath, and serve as if the point decides the match. Each accurate serve equals a success; misses count as losses. Try to "win" a best-of-seven series by landing five of seven serves.

Between serves, mentally and physically reset. Note tendencies under stress—does your toss drift, or does your timing change? Adjust accordingly.

Pro Tips from the Court

Establish a repeatable pre-serve ritual: same breath, same routine. This anchors the mind during tension. Use positive self-talk to replace doubt.

Take It Up a Notch

Add distractions—background noise, teammates clapping, or time limits—to simulate match intensity. Rotate servers through scenarios to mimic real rotations.

Common Mistakes & Fixes

- **Mistake:** Rushing the routine.
    - **Fix:** Slow down; perform the identical pre-serve sequence each time.
- **Mistake:** Over-swinging.
    - **Fix:** Trust mechanics; focus on contact quality.
- **Mistake:** Negative self-talk.
    - **Fix:** Replace with affirmations like "smooth toss, clean hit."

Benchmarks by Level

- **Beginner:** 5 of 10 serves accurately under quiet conditions.
- **Intermediate:** 6 of 10 under time or noise pressure.
- **Advanced:** 8 of 10 accurate during live scrimmage or distraction drills.

How This Connects

With serving fundamentals and mental focus reinforced, the next phase moves into front-row defense and timing at the net.

The mental discipline learned here reinforces confidence in every future serving scenario and complements Drill 1 – Serving with Purpose.

Coach's Note

Treat pressure like a skill, not a feeling. Every serve is a chance to practice composure, even when your pulse rises.

Drill 7: Block Jump Timing

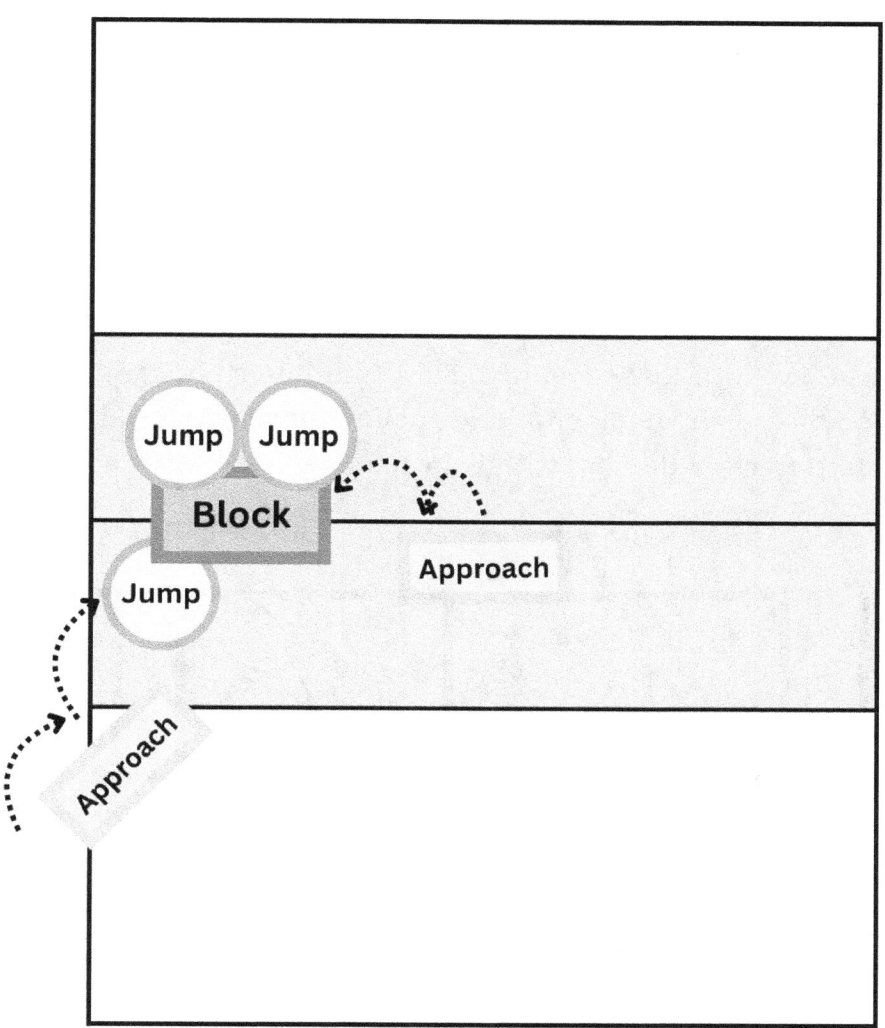

Figure 7. Blocker and hitter timing sequence illustrating approach steps and jump alignment at the net.

Primary Roles: Middles, front-row hitters, blockers.

Why This Matters

Effective blocking is about anticipation and timing, not just height. This drill trains players to read the hitter's motion and jump in rhythm to meet the ball at its peak.

What You'll Need

A net, a partner acting as a hitter, and markers for footwork positioning.

Let's Do It

Start stationary at the net in a loaded stance. Have the hitter perform approach motions while you practice reading their shoulder and arm cues. Once comfortable, add real hits or tosses. Time your jump to clear the net, with your hands slightly forward to block the ball's trajectory.

Pro Tips from the Court

Watch the hitter's shoulder rotation—it reveals swing timing better than the ball does. Keep your hands firm but relaxed, with fingers spread wide.

Take It Up a Notch

Add movement: begin a few feet off the net and execute swing-block footwork into position. Introduce random hit locations for reaction training.

Common Mistakes & Fixes

- **Mistake:** Jumping too early.
  - **Fix:** Wait until the hitter's elbow draws back before takeoff.
- **Mistake:** Hands too vertical.
  - **Fix:** Penetrate over the net, not straight up.

Benchmarks by Level

- **Beginner:** 7 of 10 properly-timed dry jumps.
- **Intermediate:** 6 of 10 successful ball contacts.
- **Advanced:** Consistent timing against live hitters.

How This Connects

Having built timing and anticipation at the net, the following drill focuses on teamwork and recovery after contact.

This defensive timing leads into Drill 8 – Coverage Chaos, where reading and reacting quickly determine point recovery.

Drill 8: Coverage Chaos

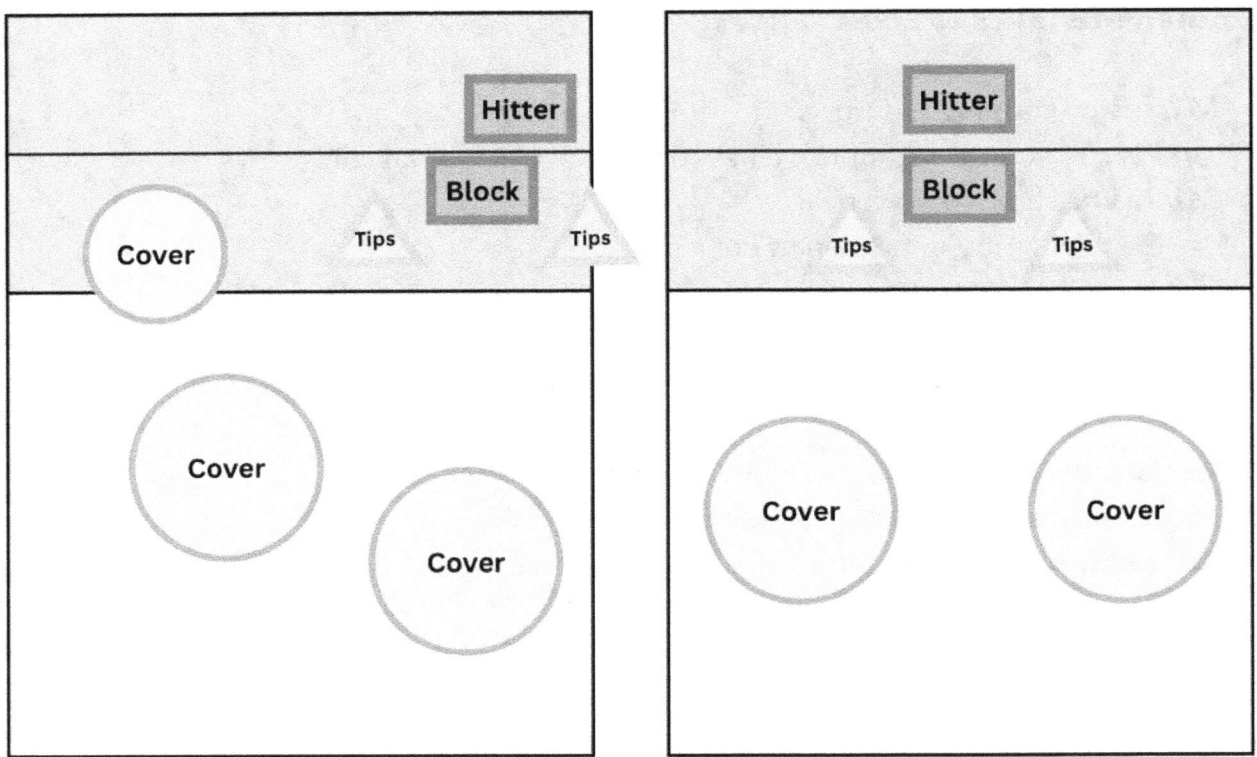

Figure 8. Coverage positions around a hitter, with arrows indicating reaction paths to blocked or deflected balls.

Primary Roles: Hitters, liberos, defensive specialists.

Why This Matters

Strong coverage turns blocked or deflected attacks into second chances. This drill builds communication, quick reactions, and spatial awareness near the hitter.

Ideal for hitters and liberos, this drill strengthens coordination between front-row attackers and their coverage teammates, reinforcing the habit of staying ready for blocked returns.

What You'll Need

Three to four players (one hitter and coverage teammates), a coach or tosser, and markers for coverage zones.

Let's Do It

As the hitter attacks, the coach blocks or deflects the ball back. Coverage players stay low and ready around the hitter, reacting instantly to dig or control the rebound. Rotate positions after every few swings.

Pro Tips from the Court

Keep your eyes on the hitter through the swing. Stay tight to the attack zone but clear the hitter's landing space. Communicate assignments before each rep.

Take It Up a Notch

Use a live blocker returning balls at variable angles. Score points for every recovered deflection to add urgency.

Common Mistakes & Fixes

- **Mistake:** Standing too upright.

- **Fix:** Lower stance, weight forward.
- **Mistake:** Overcrowding the hitter.
  - **Fix:** Maintain a 1–2 meter buffer for safety.

Benchmarks by Level

- **Beginner:** 50% successful recoveries.
- **Intermediate:** 70% recoveries with clean digs.
- **Advanced:** 85% recoveries during live hitting drills.

How This Connects

With communication and coverage strengthened, players are ready to apply those reactions to controlled offensive transitions.

Mastering coverage reinforces the recovery skills needed for Drill 9 – First Ball Side-Out, ensuring team coordination on unpredictable plays.

Coach's Note

Championship rallies are often won by second chances. Hustle for every deflection—your effort turns chaos into control.

Drill 9: First Ball Side-Out

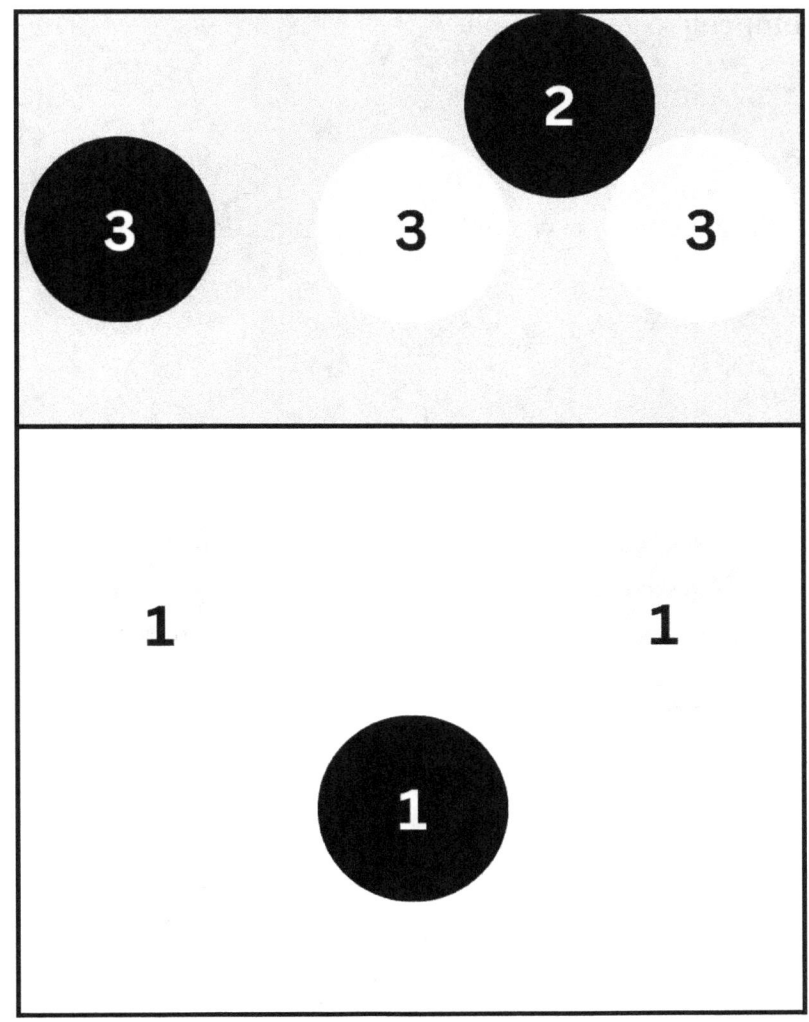

Figure 9. Two-phase first-ball side-out drill: serve-receive sequence followed by side-out scoring setup.

Primary Roles: Hitters, setters, middles.

Why This Matters

Winning the point on the first ball received—called a side-out—shifts momentum immediately. This two-phase drill first isolates the technical elements of serve-receive, then applies them in a competitive game format.

What You'll Need

Full or half court, 3–6 players, a server or ball machine, and a scoring method.

Let's Do It

- **Phase 1 – Skill Focus**: Work on serve-receive mechanics. The server delivers controlled balls; passers aim to deliver to the setter's target zone. The setter then delivers an accurate set, and the hitter attacks the designated target areas.
- **Phase 2 – Game Application**: Transition to live serves. The team must score directly from that first possession. Each successful side-out equals a point.

Pro Tips from the Court

Encourage aggression and tempo. First contacts should be confident, not cautious. Communication from passers and setters determines flow.

Take It Up a Notch

Set a four-minute timer or first-to-ten scoring goal. Rotate players after every three reps to simulate realistic lineup changes.

Common Mistakes & Fixes

- **Mistake:** Playing passively on serve-receive.
    - **Fix:** Attack mindset—step toward the ball.
- **Mistake:** Delayed transitions between phases.
    - **Fix:** Reset quickly; treat every ball as live play.

Benchmarks by Level

- **Beginner:** 5 successful side-outs in 10 attempts.
- **Intermediate:** 8 of 10 successful side-outs with consistent tempo.
- **Advanced:** 10 consecutive side-outs against unpredictable serves.

How This Connects

After mastering first-ball efficiency, the next section enhances team passing systems and serve-receive rotations.

Executing first-ball offense seamlessly prepares athletes for Drill 11 – Transition Attack, emphasizing speed from defense to offense. Once athletes can consistently score off the first ball, they're ready to strengthen defensive transition and counterattack speed in the next phase — Drill 10: Serve-Receive Circuits.

Drill 10: Serve-Receive Circuits

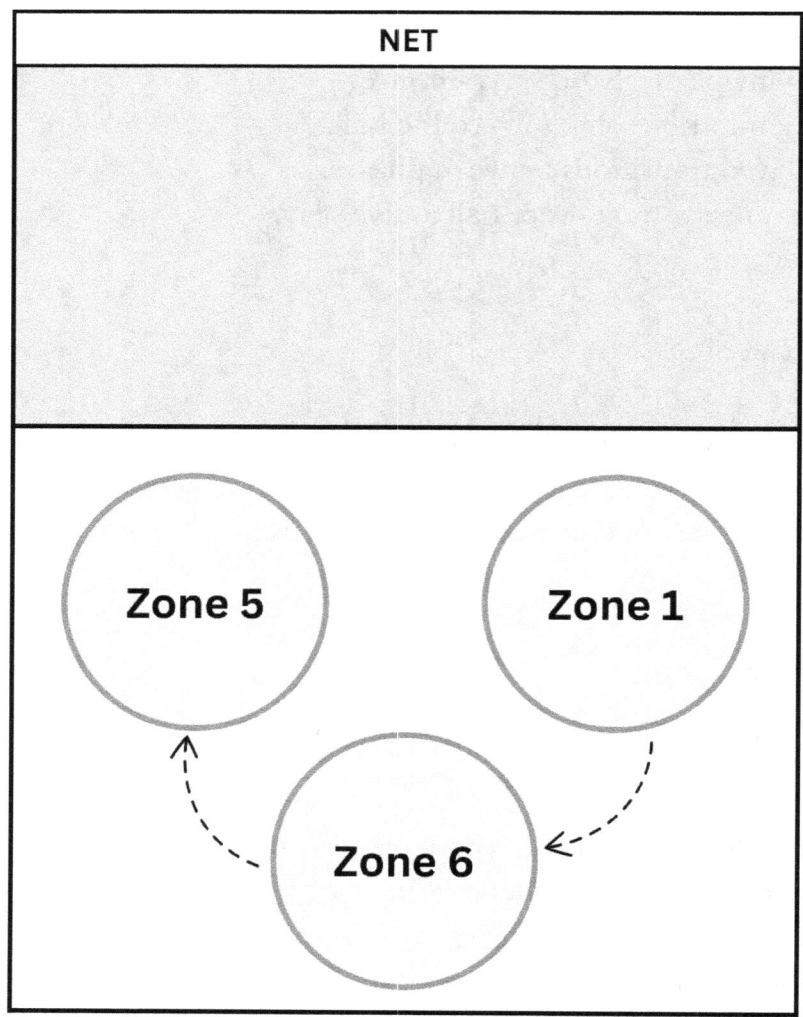

Figure 10. Serve-receive rotation pattern with passers moving through multiple court zones.

Primary Roles: Liberos, outside hitters, defensive specialists.

Why This Matters

Serve-receive is the foundation of offensive rhythm. The ability to read the serve, move decisively, and communicate clearly determines how effectively a team can launch an attack. This drill builds stamina, consistency, and confidence across multiple formations while training athletes to handle unpredictability.

This drill is most beneficial for liberos and outside hitters, who must maintain composure in serve-receive while coordinating with setters and attackers under pressure.

What You'll Need

Three to six players, one server or a ball machine, cones or tape to mark serve zones, and a clipboard or simple rotation chart. Optional: stopwatch or timer for pacing.

Let's Do It

Divide the back row into three passing lanes (zones 1, 6, 5). The server delivers balls to random zones. After every five serves, players rotate one position to the left so everyone experiences each angle.

Track how many clean passes land in the setter's target zone before rotation. Run three complete circuits—roughly fifteen total serves per athlete.

Pro Tips from the Court

Stay balanced and low throughout the movement. Read the server's toss and body line to anticipate direction. Call "mine" early to prevent hesitation in crossover zones. Finish each pass by holding your platform steady toward the target.

Take It Up a Notch

Add a setter and a hitter so every accurate pass flows into a live play. Increase server intensity or introduce float serves to challenge tracking skills. For competitive focus, assign team points for each perfect pass-set sequence.

Common Mistakes & Fixes

- **Mistake:** Waiting flat-footed for the serve.
  - **Fix:** Keep weight slightly forward on the balls of your feet; use split-step timing as the serve is struck.
- **Mistake:** Colliding in crossover zones.
  - **Fix:** Clarify verbal cues before each round and trust the caller's command.
- **Mistake:** Over-rotating arms on contact.
  - **Fix:** Drive through the ball with legs and shoulders, not forearm swing.

Benchmarks by Level

- **Beginner:** 10 clean passes out of 15 serves per circuit.
- **Intermediate:** 12 clean passes with no more than one communication error.
- **Advanced:** 13 or more accurate passes against live or jump serves.

How This Connects

Once serve-receive consistency is established, the upcoming drills combine these skills—defense, transition, and attack—into more complete, game-ready sequences.

Serve-receive circuits reinforce the passing discipline required for Drill 9 – First Ball Side-Out and establish consistency under repetition that fuels long-term match endurance.

Drill 11: Transition Attack

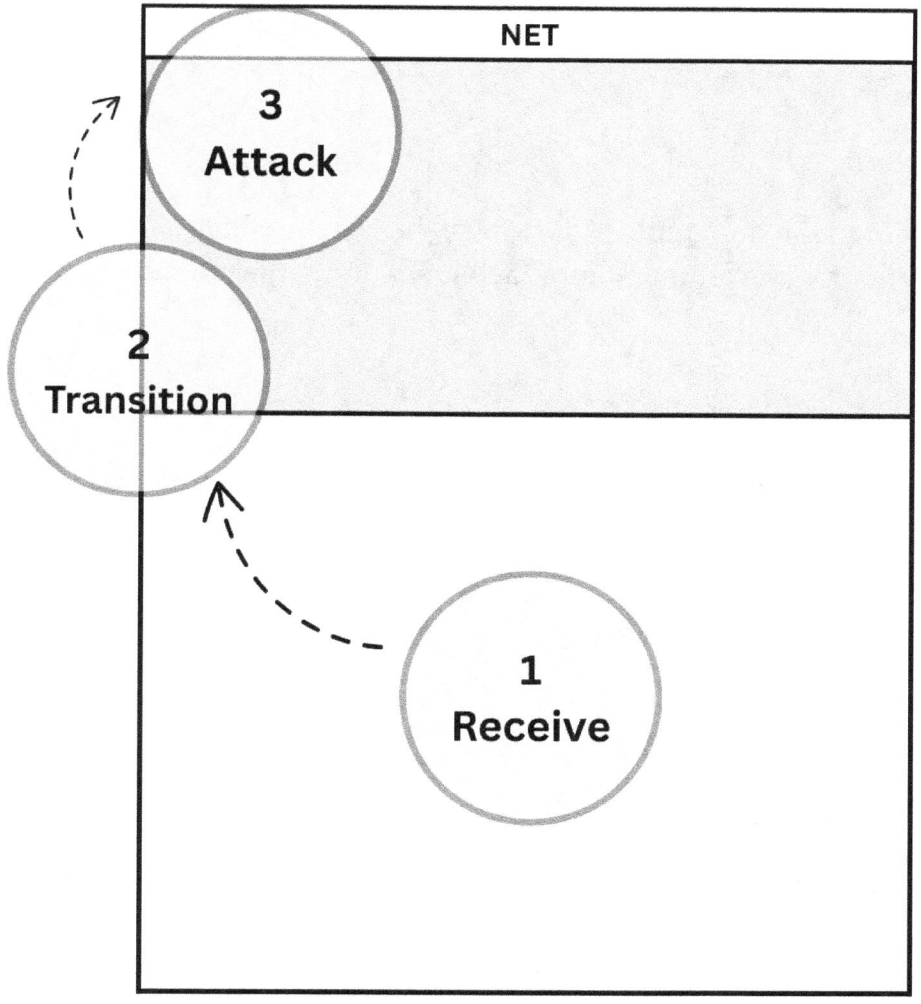

Figure 11. Transition drill illustrating dig, movement off the net, and attack path during defensive recovery.

Primary Roles: Setters, hitters, all players.

Why This Matters

Most points are earned not on the first play, but after a defensive save forces transition. Great teams convert defense into offense instantly. This drill builds that conversion speed—training defenders to recover, reposition, and attack efficiently while tired.

What You'll Need

Full or half court, a coach or partner to toss or hit the first ball, a setter, and one to two hitters. Cones or floor tape can mark approach lanes and target zones.

Let's Do It

The coach tosses or hits a ball to the defender. After the dig, the defender quickly transitions off the net, resets footwork, and calls for the set. The setter delivers a hittable ball, and the player completes an attack into the target area.

Run ten continuous reps, switching digger and hitter roles every five. Keep transitions quick—no pauses between digs.

Pro Tips from the Court

Eyes up immediately after the dig. Many players watch the ball too long instead of moving into the approach position. Explode off the net with short, efficient steps. Setters should prioritize height and tempo over perfection. Hitters should time their approach with the ball's release, not just the setter's hands.

Take It Up a Notch

Make it live: defenders dig real spikes and instantly transition to attack. Add blockers or blockers-plus-defense for full-rally simulation. Track successful transition kills versus errors to monitor improvement.

Common Mistakes & Fixes

- **Mistake:** Delayed movement after the dig.
    - **Fix:** Create a trigger cue—first contact equals instant retreat step.
- **Mistake:** Drifting approaches.
    - **Fix:** Mark consistent start lines with tape; emphasize linear momentum toward the net.
- **Mistake:** Fatigue-reducing power.
    - **Fix:** Focus on efficient footwork and core engagement rather than swing force alone.

Benchmarks by Level

- **Beginner:** 5 accurate transition attacks in 10 reps.
- **Intermediate:** 7 successful in-bounds attacks with a controlled approach.
- **Advanced:** 9 successful kills out of 10 under live-ball conditions.

How This Connects

Transition attack builds on the defensive control and quick resets trained in earlier drills. By learning to convert digs into purposeful offense, you prepare for the upcoming system-based drills that emphasize teamwork, communication, and extended rally decision-making.

This drill strengthens the link between defense and offense, setting you up for more advanced game-flow scenarios in the next section.

Coach's Note

The best players master what happens between plays. Transition quickly, breathe, and reset—momentum belongs to the team that moves first.

Drill 12: Defensive Read & Reaction

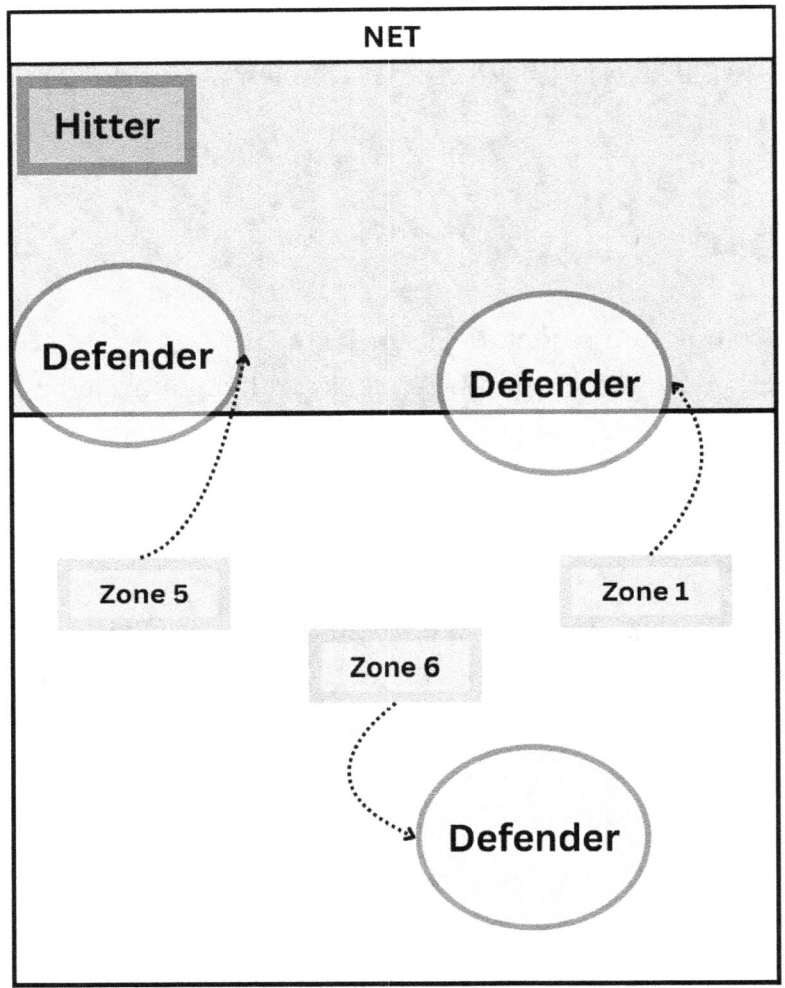

Figure 12. Defensive read sequence showing movement from base position to dig coverage across Zones 5, 6, and 1.

Primary Roles: Liberos, defensive specialists, all players.

Why This Matters

Defense starts before the ball is ever struck. The ability to read the hitter's body—shoulder angle, arm speed, and approach path—allows defenders to react sooner and position themselves where the ball will go, not where it already is. This drill trains athletes to interpret cues, move decisively, and improve first-contact control under live-hit conditions.

What You'll Need

- One to two hitters and a coach or partner to toss.
- At least one defender in the back row (rotate multiple players as needed).
- 6–10 volleyballs.
- A net and court space with clearly marked Zones 5, 6, and 1 for target tracking.

Let's Do It

1. **Start Position**: The defender begins in base position—knees bent, weight forward, balanced over the balls of the feet, approximately 10–15 ft (3–4.5 m) behind the attack line.
2. **Visual Cue Phase**: The coach or toss partner sends a ball to the hitter. The defender must watch the hitter's shoulder and elbow to anticipate the direction of the attack.
3. **Reaction Phase**: As the hitter swings, the defender takes a small adjustment step and executes a controlled dig toward Zone 3 (setter's area).
4. **Reset and Repeat**: Perform 10 balls per round, rotating attack angles (left, middle, right). Complete three rounds.

For added focus, have the defender call out the intended zone before contact—this forces visual reading instead of guessing.

Pro Tips from the Court

- Watch the shoulder rotation, not the ball toss—the shoulder reveals the true attack line.
- Keep arms relaxed until you see the swing path, then lock in the platform angle as you move.
- Anticipate the trajectory based on approach speed: fast approach = sharp angle; slow approach = roll shot.
- Stay low and ready—reacting up is quicker than reacting down.

Take It Up a Notch

Add a second hitter to simulate decision-making under pressure. Defenders must read which attacker receives the set and adjust instantly. For advanced teams, alternate attack types (spike, tip, roll) to train pattern recognition.

Track reaction time by measuring how early the defender shifts compared to contact—aim to move before the swing finishes.

Common Mistakes & Fixes

- **Mistake:** Watching the ball instead of the hitter.
    - **Fix:** Focus eyes on the hitter's torso and arm through the approach.
- **Mistake:** Standing too upright.
    - **Fix:** Lower hips; maintain nose-over-toes posture.
- **Mistake:** Reacting after impact.
    - **Fix:** Train to read body language earlier—shoulder turn signals direction.

Benchmarks by Level

- **Beginner:** Correct reads on 6 of 10 hits; controlled dig toward the target zone.
- **Intermediate:** 8 of 10 successful reads and digs across multiple angles.
- **Advanced:** Consistent anticipation before contact with 90% dig success in live play.

How This Connects

Mastering visual reading and reaction creates defensive anticipation that feeds directly into Drill 13 – Dig & Cover Circuit, where players apply those reads while moving through multiple defensive positions.

Coach's Note

Elite defenders don't guess—they observe. Every approach tells a story. Train your eyes to read the hitter's shoulder like words on a page, and you'll react before others even see the swing.

Drill 13: Dig & Cover Circuit

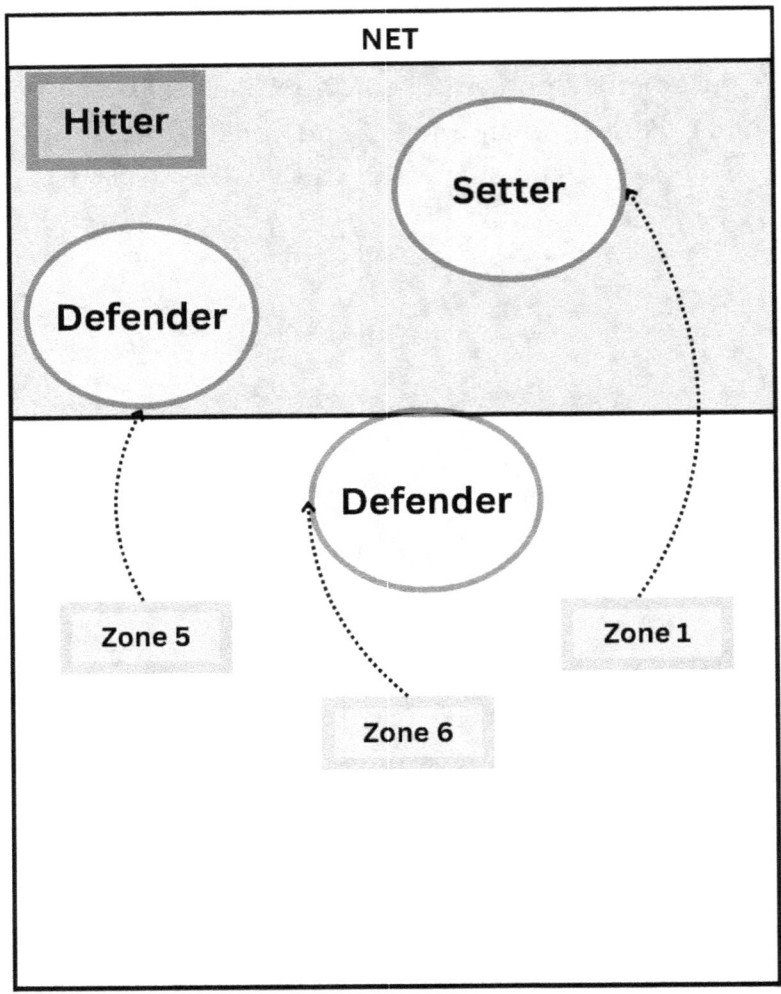

Figure 13. Dig-and-cover rotation illustrating continuous movement between coverage and defensive positions across Zones 5 and 6.

Primary Roles: Liberos, setters, hitters, all players.

Why This Matters

Defense doesn't end with one dig—it continues through recovery and coverage. This circuit drill reinforces continuous motion, helping players stay active after contact, reposition for rebounds, and maintain rhythm during long rallies. It trains reaction, endurance, and teamwork under sustained defensive pressure.

What You'll Need

- A net and full half-court setup.
- Two hitters, one setter, two defenders (minimum)
- 6–10 volleyballs.
- Markers for coverage zones near Zones 2, 3, and 4.

Let's Do It

1. Start with one hitter attacking from Zone 4 (left front). Two defenders cover Zones 5 and 6 (15 ft / 4.5 m back from the net).
2. Defender 1 digs the first attack to the setter; Defender 2 rotates forward to cover tip range.
3. After each dig, players switch positions—cover → dig → set → cover—creating a continuous cycle.
4. Run for 45 seconds of nonstop play, then rotate hitters and defenders. Complete 3 rounds.

Pro Tips from the Court

- Stay low and balanced—quick recoveries start from the hips, not the knees.
- Call "mine" early to reduce hesitation.
- Watch the hitter's off-speed touch; coverage players should creep closer as the arm slows.

Take It Up a Notch

Add a third attacker alternating between Zones 2 and 4 so defenders must shift and react to different angles. Time each round and set goals for total controlled digs (for example, 15 clean contacts in 45 seconds).

Common Mistakes & Fixes

- **Mistake:** Standing after the first dig.
  - **Fix:** Reset stance immediately after contact.
- **Mistake:** No communication on coverage.
  - **Fix:** Assign zones and use verbal cues like "tip," "block," or "deep."
- **Mistake:** Over-extending on dives.
  - **Fix:** Slide through contact and recover on knees for a faster reset.

Benchmarks by Level

- **Beginner:** 8 clean digs per round.
- **Intermediate:** 12 digs and 3 coverage recoveries per round.
- **Advanced:** 18 successful defensive contacts with minimal errors in 45 seconds.

How This Connects

This drill cements defensive mobility and awareness, laying the foundation for Drill 14 – Setter Decision Challenge, where players transition from dig to offense under pressure.

Coach's Note

A good defense doesn't rest after the dig—movement after contact defines elite players. Finish every play ready for the next ball.

Drill 14: Setter Decision Challenge

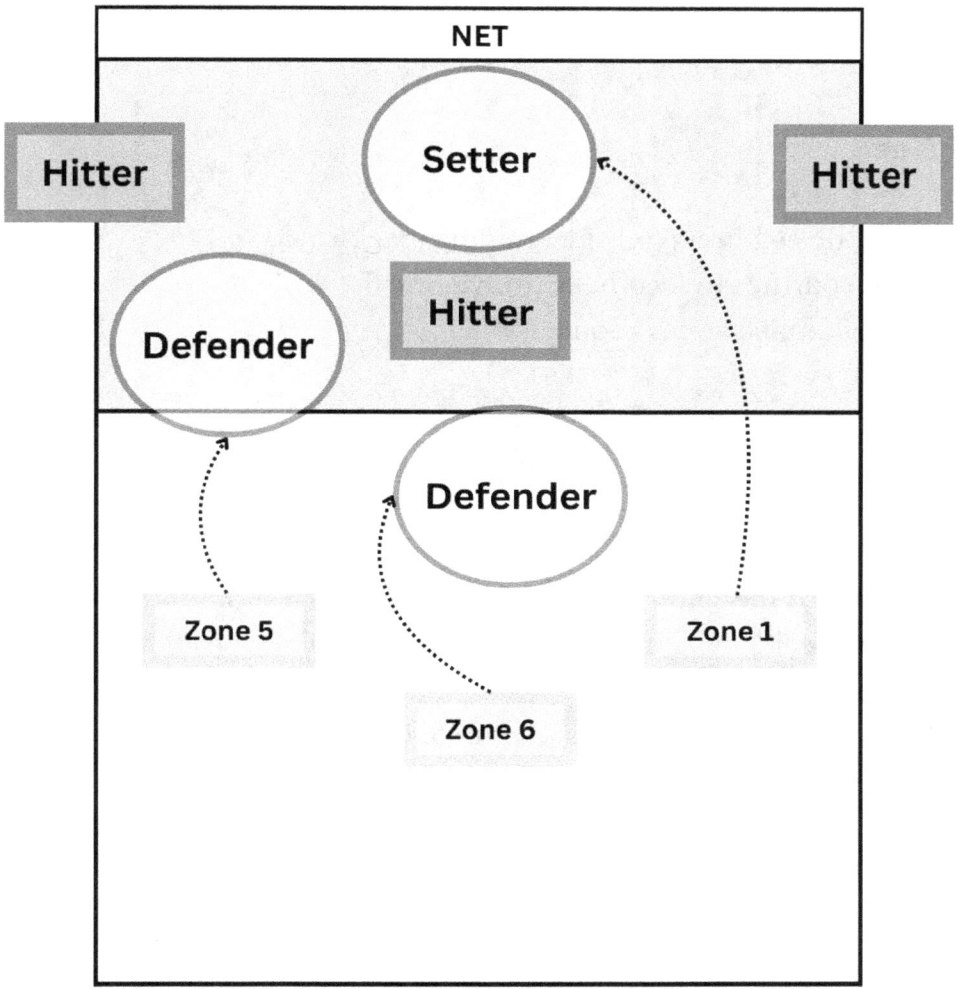

Figure 14. Setter-decision pattern showing reads and set options to outside, middle, and back-row attackers.

Primary Roles: Setters, hitters, all players.

Why This Matters

Smart setting decisions separate great teams from good ones. This drill teaches setters to read the block, recognize defensive gaps, and choose the right attacker under time constraints. It builds court vision, tempo control, and tactical confidence.

What You'll Need

- One setter and three hitters (outside, middle, back-row).
- A coach or toss partner to feed balls from Zone 6.
- Net and marked attack zones (Zone 4, 3, 2).
- 10 volleyballs.

Let's Do It

1. The coach tosses to the setter from the backcourt (18 ft / 5.5 m off the net).
2. The setter must decide which hitter to set based on block position (called out by the coach each rep).
3. Hitters execute their attack and reset immediately.
4. After 10 sets, rotate hitters and repeat with different block scenarios.

Encourage setters to read before the toss—use peripheral vision to locate blockers and defenders.

Pro Tips from the Court

- Trust your first read—hesitation kills tempo.
- Keep hands high and neutral until decision is made.
- Communicate with hitters: tempo calls like "quick," "go," or "pipe" create rhythm.
- Use a quiet body—no extra motion before contact.

Take It Up a Notch

Add a live blocker on each pin so the setter must make real-time decisions. Track success rate (percentage of unblocked attacks). For advanced groups, add back-row defenders and score points for kills resulting from smart decisions.

Common Mistakes & Fixes

- **Mistake:** Predetermined sets.
    - **Fix:** Train to read block posture before release.
- **Mistake:** Low set trajectory.
    - **Fix:** Emphasize full extension and wrist flick at release.
- **Mistake:** No communication with hitters.
    - **Fix:** Call tempo and location before contact.

Benchmarks by Level

- **Beginner:** 7 of 10 sets accurately placed with basic reads.
- **Intermediate:** 8 of 10 effective decisions with varied block formations.
- **Advanced:** 9 of 10 unblocked sets under live defensive pressure.

How This Connects

This drill bridges defense and offense, preparing players for Drill 15 – Attack Coverage & Continuation, where smart decisions flow into follow-through and team coordination after each hit.

Coach's Note

Setters are the team's strategists. Think two steps ahead—your best set is the one that keeps the block guessing.

Drill 15: Attack Coverage & Continuation

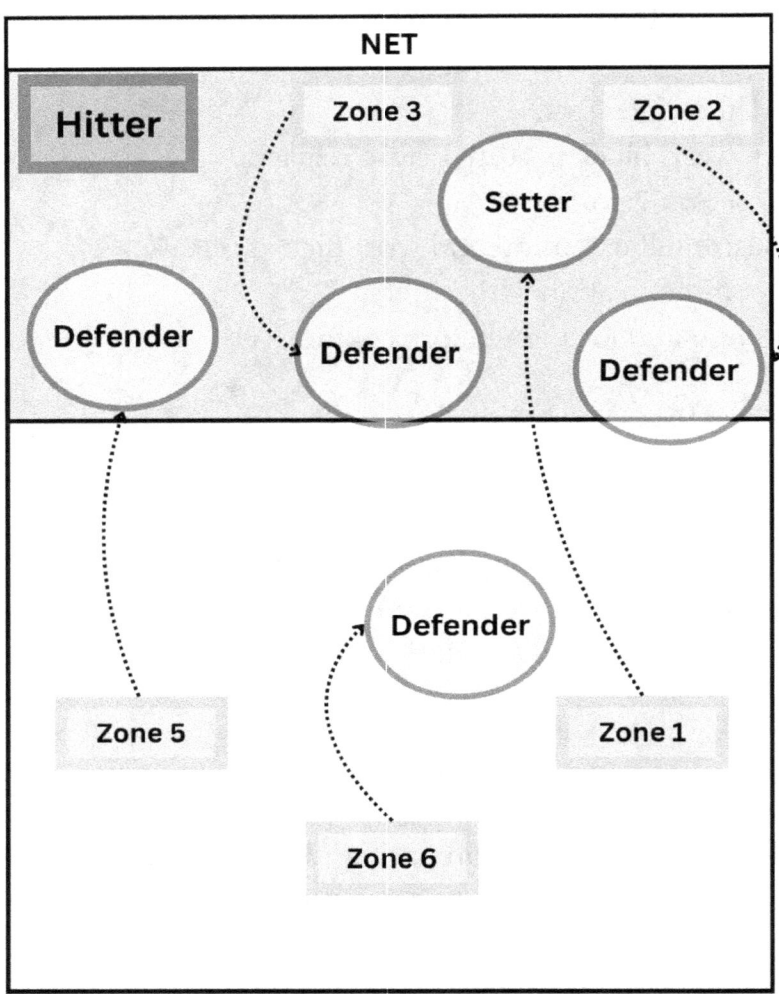

Figure 15. Coverage triangle around attacker illustrating defensive positions and movement after a blocked ball.

Primary Roles: Hitters, liberos, defensive specialists, all players.

Why This Matters

Even the best hit can be blocked. Teams that win rallies know how to cover and continue after contact. This drill teaches attackers and defenders to stay engaged after the swing, turning blocked shots into second-chance points.

What You'll Need

- A net and half-court setup.
- 1 hitter, 1 setter, and 2 coverage players.
- 6–8 volleyballs.
- Cones or tape marking coverage zones (5 ft / 1.5 m radius around hitter).

Let's Do It

1. The hitter executes an attack from Zone 4 while two teammates position for coverage.
2. The coach or partner blocks or deflects the ball deliberately.
3. Coverage players recover the ball and reset the offense—the setter delivers a second set for a follow-up hit.
4. Complete 10 sequences, rotating hitters and coverage positions each round.

Pro Tips from the Court

- Stay clear of the hitter's landing space.
- Anticipate deflections by watching the blockers' hands.
- Pass high and center to reset quickly.
- Communication is key—coverage players call 'got it' to avoid collisions.

Take It Up a Notch

Add a second blocker and a live defense to simulate real game continuations. Award a point for each successful re-attack that results in a controlled swing. Track success rate per 10 balls.

Common Mistakes & Fixes

- **Mistake:** Standing still after hitting.
  - **Fix:** Practice landing and immediately turning to cover.
- **Mistake:** Coverage too close to the net.
  - **Fix:** Maintain 5–7 ft (1.5–2 m) depth for reaction time.
- **Mistake:** No second tempo on follow-up.
  - **Fix:** Set quicker to capitalize on disorganized defense.

Benchmarks by Level

- **Beginner:** Recover 5 of 10 blocked balls into controlled sets.
- **Intermediate:** 7 of 10 recovered into attackable sets.
- **Advanced:** 9 of 10 successful recoveries with scoring continuation.

How This Connects

This coverage work prepares teams for Drill 16 – Team Serve-Receive Rotation, where players apply communication and coordination in a full six-player system.

Coach's Note

Don't watch your hit—follow it. Great teams expect the block and plan the next move before the ball comes down.

Drill 16: Team Serve-Receive Rotation

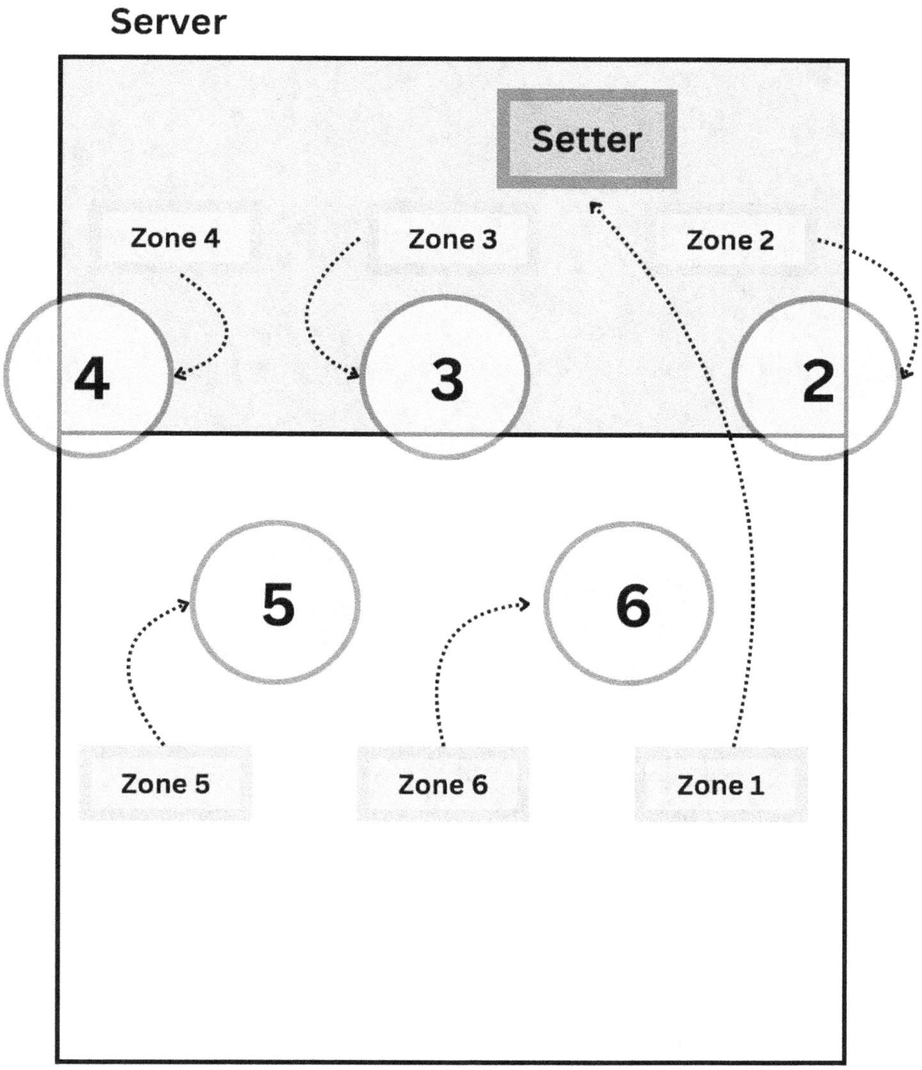

Figure 16. Full-rotation serve-receive positions showing player movement and target zones across the court.

Primary Roles: All positions.

Why This Matters

Serve-receive success depends on rhythm, spacing, and trust. This full-rotation drill simulates live-match situations so players practice moving, communicating, and executing clean first contacts in an actual game rotation. It strengthens coordination and composure in every lineup.

What You'll Need

- Full court and net.
- Six players (minimum) plus server and coach or toss partner.
- 10 volleyballs.
- Markers for zones and serve targets.

Let's Do It

1. Arrange six players in their serve-receive formation. The server serves from Zone 1 to designated target areas.
2. The team passes, sets, and attacks as in live play.
3. After each rally, rotate clockwise to the next serve-receive formation until all six positions have served and received.
4. Track passing accuracy (three-point scale) and rotation communication quality after each round (three-point scale: 3 = perfect pass to the setter's target zone; 2 = playable pass that keeps the rally alive; 1 = off-target pass requiring scrambling; 0 = error or unplayable ball).

Pro Tips from the Court

- Keep hands up for visibility and call "mine" early.
- Rotate quickly between points to mimic game tempo.

- Back-row players anchor spacing; front-row players should avoid drifting into serve-receive lanes.

Take It Up a Notch

Use two servers alternating sides for realistic angles. Add pressure by scoring each rotation (10 points possible; 1 point per perfect pass). Advanced groups can set time limits (60 seconds per rotation) to simulate tournament pace.

Common Mistakes & Fixes

- **Mistake:** Players forget rotational zones.
    - **Fix:** Mark positions with floor tape until spacing is automatic.
- **Mistake:** No communication on short serves.
    - **Fix:** Assign specific roles for each serve angle.
- **Mistake:** Static movement after a pass.
    - **Fix:** Encourage players to transition immediately to attack or coverage.

Benchmarks by Level

- **Beginner:** The team achieves 60% perfect passes through two rotations.
- **Intermediate:** 75% perfect passes with smooth communication.
- **Advanced:** 85% or higher accuracy across all six rotations.

How This Connects

Completing serve-receive rotations prepares the team for Drill 17 – Quick Offense Coordination, where those clean first contacts translate into faster, more efficient attacks.

Coach's Note

A team that can receive under pressure can control any match. Trust your rotation and move as one unit.

Drill 17: Quick Offense Coordination

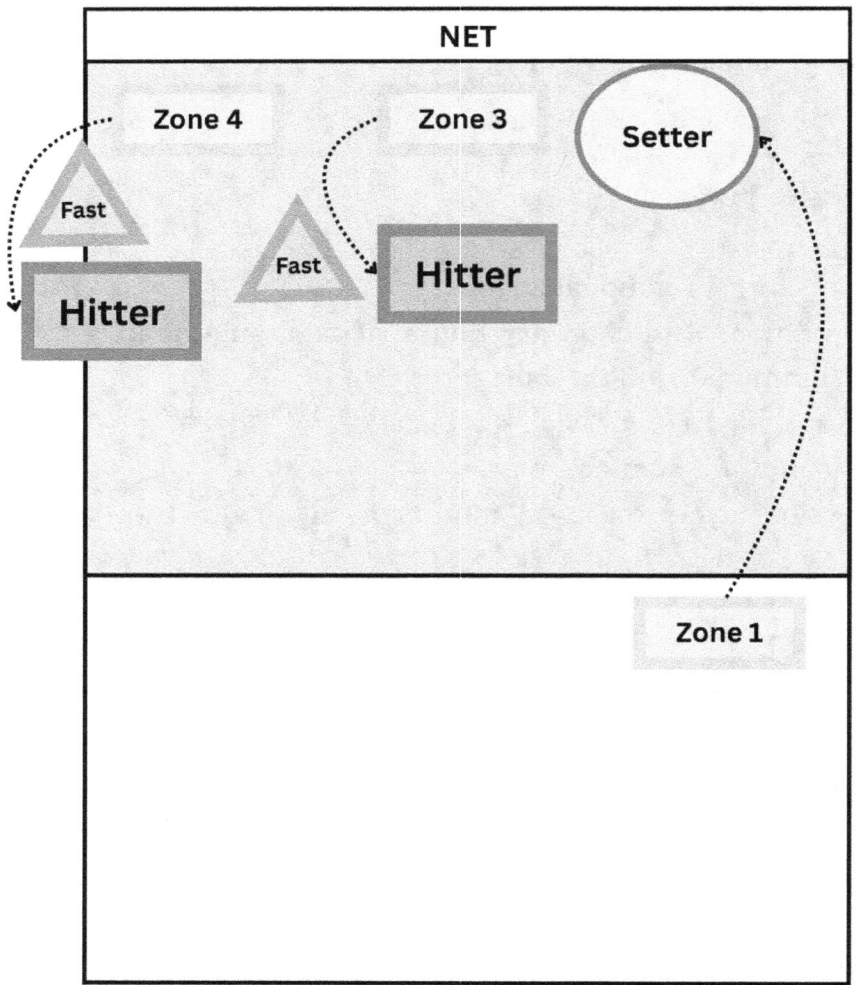

Figure 17. Setter-to-hitter tempo diagram showing approach timing and set trajectory for quick offense attacks.

Primary Roles: Setters, middles, hitters.

Why This Matters

Fast-tempo offense keeps blockers off balance and forces defenses to react late. This drill sharpens setter-hitter timing, improves footwork precision, and teaches players to synchronize approaches with a quicker ball release.

What You'll Need

- One setter and two hitters (middle and outside).
- Coach or feeder with 10–12 volleyballs.
- Full net setup with blocking pads (optional).

Let's Do It

1. The hitter starts 5–6 ft (1.5–1.8 m) off the net and times their approach to meet the set at its peak.
2. The setter initiates rapid-tempo sets (about 0.5 seconds faster than normal rhythm).
3. After each hit, reset immediately and repeat 10 times per hitter.
4. Focus on rhythm—the approach starts as the ball leaves the setter's hands.

Pro Tips from the Court

- Communicate the set height with consistent tempo calls.
- Keep sets just above the antenna to maintain speed and control.
- The hitter's last two steps should explode forward, not upward.
- The middle hitters should keep their eyes on the setter's hands, not the ball.

Take It Up a Notch

Add a live blocker and defensive line to force setters to adjust tempos based on open angles. Track time between set release and attack contact using a stopwatch (goal: under 1.3 seconds).

Common Mistakes & Fixes

- **Mistake:** Early jump by the hitter.
    - **Fix:** Count rhythm aloud—"1-2-up"—to sync footwork with the set.
- **Mistake:** The setter floats the ball too high.
    - **Fix:** Push forward through wrist extension for faster tempo.
- **Mistake:** No verbal cue.
    - **Fix:** Call set type before contact to align timing.

Benchmarks by Level

- **Beginner:** 5 of 10 successful quick hits with proper tempo.
- **Intermediate:** 7 of 10 fast tempos landing in target zones.
- **Advanced:** 9 of 10 attacks executed within 1 to 3 seconds of set release.

How This Connects

Consistent timing in fast offense leads directly into Drill 18 – Serve & Transition Defense, where players switch from offensive momentum to defensive readiness without hesitation.

Coach's Note

Speed is nothing without rhythm. Fast offense works only when everyone trusts the same beat.

Drill 18: Serve & Transition Defense

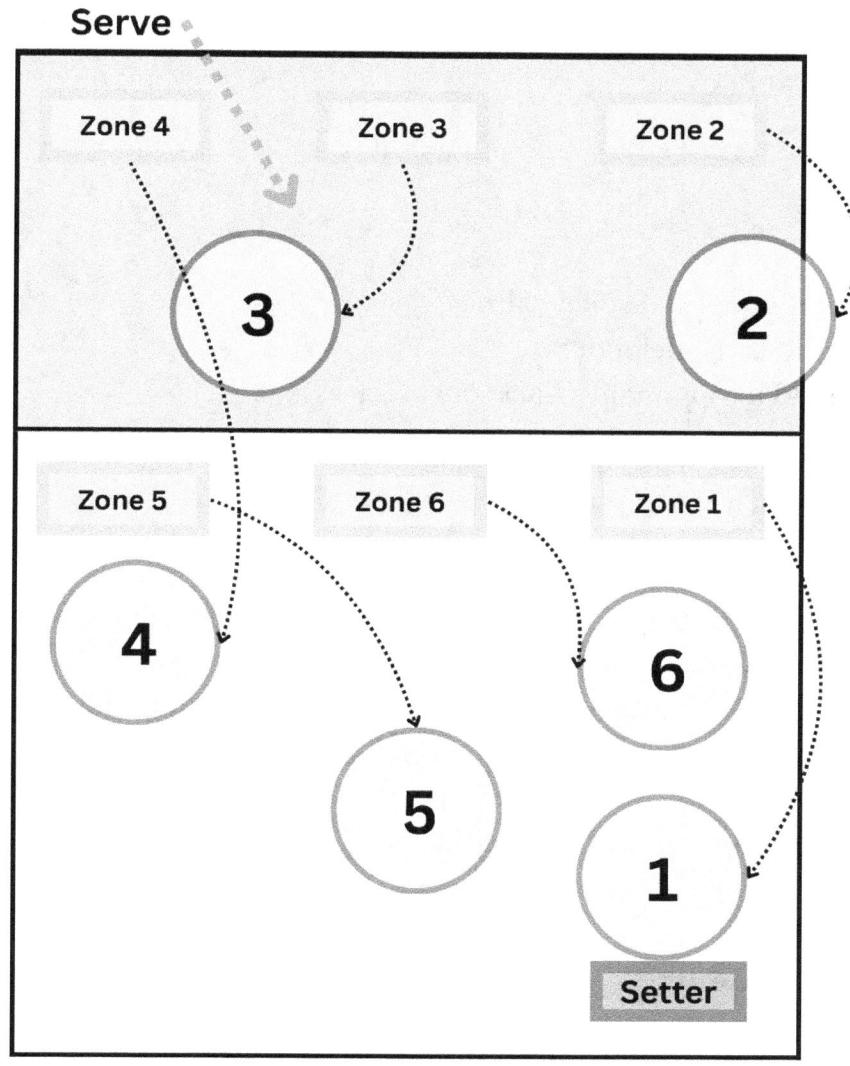

Figure 18. Serve-and-transition sequence showing movement from service line to defensive base positions across Zones 5 and 6.

Primary Roles: Servers, liberos, blockers, all players.

Why This Matters

Serving well means nothing without immediate defensive organization. This drill combines serving execution with a quick transition into team defense, building awareness and readiness for the next play.

What You'll Need

- Court with net and 6–10 volleyballs.
- One server and three defenders.
- Targets marked in opponent's backcourt zones (5, 6, 1).

Let's Do It

1. The server targets a specific zone (Zone 5 short, Zone 1 deep). After contact, the sever immediately steps into the defensive base (15–20 ft / 4.5–6 m off the net).
2. The coach or partner initiates a return ball to simulate an opponent's attack.
3. Defenders read and execute a dig to the setter zone (Zone 3). Reset and repeat 10 times.
4. Record serve accuracy and defensive control for each rep.

Pro Tips from the Court

- Finish your serve balanced and ready to move—avoid watching the ball after contact.
- Communicate coverage zones as you transition.
- Servers should call defense before serving ("deep 6," "short 5").

Take It Up a Notch

Add live opponents receiving and returning serves. Track how quickly your team can establish a defensive formation after each serve (goal: under 2 seconds). Award points for successful serve-and-dig combinations.

Common Mistakes & Fixes

- **Mistake:** Ball-watching after serve.
    - **Fix:** Rehearse serve-to-defense footwork without a ball.
- **Mistake:** Slow defensive setup.
    - **Fix:** Call base positions before serving to prime movement.
- **Mistake:** No zone communication.
    - **Fix:** Assign numbered calls ("Cover 1," "Deep 6").

Benchmarks by Level

- **Beginner:** 6 of 10 serves land in target zones with proper defensive transition.
- **Intermediate:** 8 of 10 serve-to-dig successes within 3 seconds.
- **Advanced:** 9 of 10 successful serve-and-defense combinations under 2 seconds.

How This Connects

Efficient serve-to-defense transitions set the tone for Drill 19 – Game Simulation: Controlled Rally, where players apply everything in sustained, live rally situations.

Coach's Note

A great serve starts the point—a great transition wins it. Always land ready to dig.

Drill 19: Game Simulation: Controlled Rally

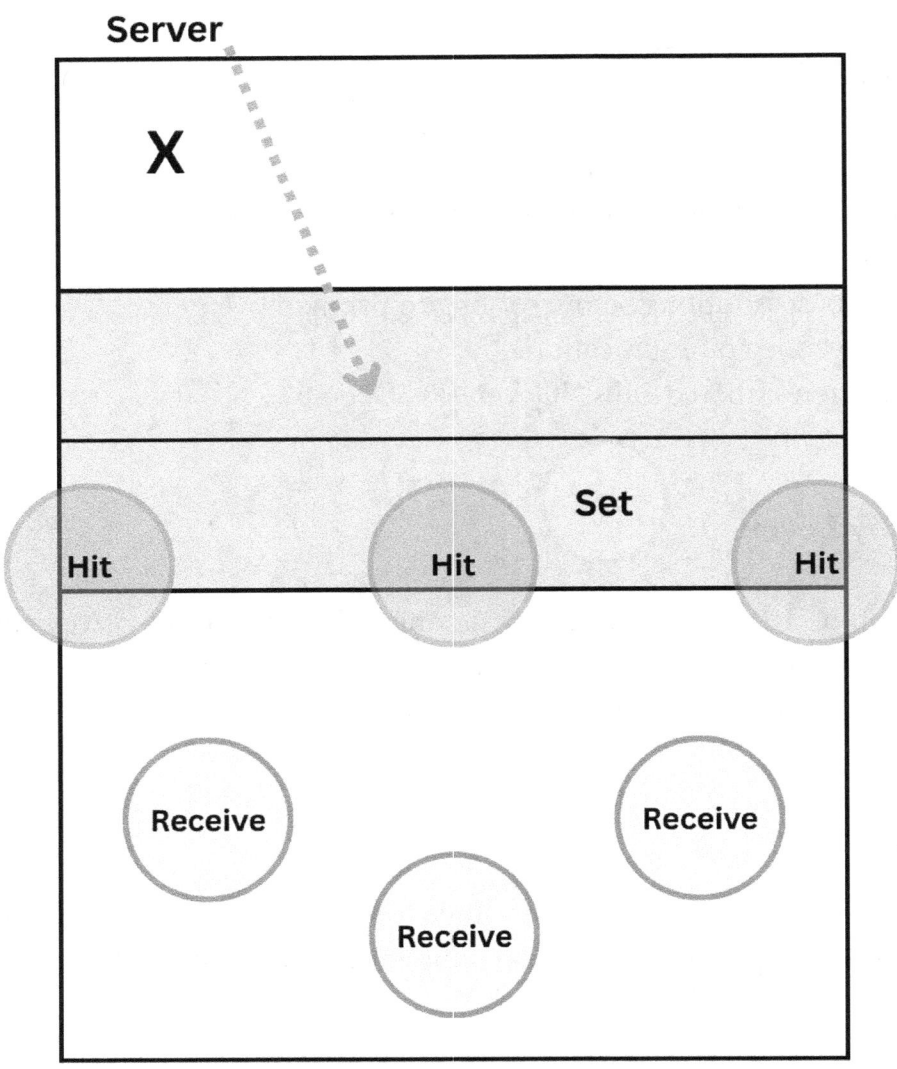

Figure 19. Controlled rally sequence illustrating sustained play transitions through serve, pass, set, attack, and reset phases.

Primary Roles: All positions.

Why This Matters

Game flow is built on rhythm, decision-making, and recovery. Controlled rally training allows athletes to link skills under real-match conditions while staying focused on ball control and communication. It bridges the gap between technical drills and competitive scrimmage.

What You'll Need

- Full court and net.
- Two teams of 6 (or fewer for small-sided versions).
- 10–12 volleyballs.
- Scoreboard or timer.

Let's Do It

1. Begin with a serve to start each rally. Teams play until one side makes an error or the ball becomes unreturnable.
2. Keep each rally within a 45-second window to emphasize continuous play and discipline.
3. Between rallies, reset rotations quickly—no more than 8 seconds—to maintain pace.
4. Coaches track total controlled contacts (passes, sets, attacks) per rally; the goal is steady tempo and smart shot selection.

Pro Tips from the Court

- Focus on placement over power during long rallies.
- Call every ball early; clear, loud communication prevents confusion.
- Read opponent hitters—anticipation saves effort.
- Keep transitions smooth: defense → offense → reset.

Take It Up a Notch

Assign point values for rally length (1 point = 10 contacts). Teams compete to reach 100 contacts first. For advanced groups, alternate objectives—one rally limited to roll shots (a soft, high-arching attack meant to land in open space), another requiring pipe attacks (a back-row attack that comes from the middle of the court), or back-row digs (defensive saves made deep in zones 5 and 6).

Common Mistakes & Fixes

- **Mistake:** Players slow down between rallies.
    - **Fix:** Use a countdown timer; build urgency.
- **Mistake:** Loss of focus after long points.
    - **Fix:** Reset with breathing cue: "Next ball."
- **Mistake:** Inconsistent tempo.
    - **Fix:** The setter maintains verbal rhythm ("go," "quick," "high").

Benchmarks by Level

- **Beginner:** Average 8-10 controlled contacts per rally.
- **Intermediate:** 15-20 contacts with consistent tempo.
- **Advanced:** 25+ contacts, sustaining control for 45 seconds or longer.

How This Connects

This drill reinforces extended play and teamwork, setting up Drill 20 – Pressure Game Scenarios, where those same habits are tested under scoreboard stress.

Coach's Note

Control the chaos. A calm team in a long rally owns the momentum every time.

Drill 20: Pressure Game Scenarios

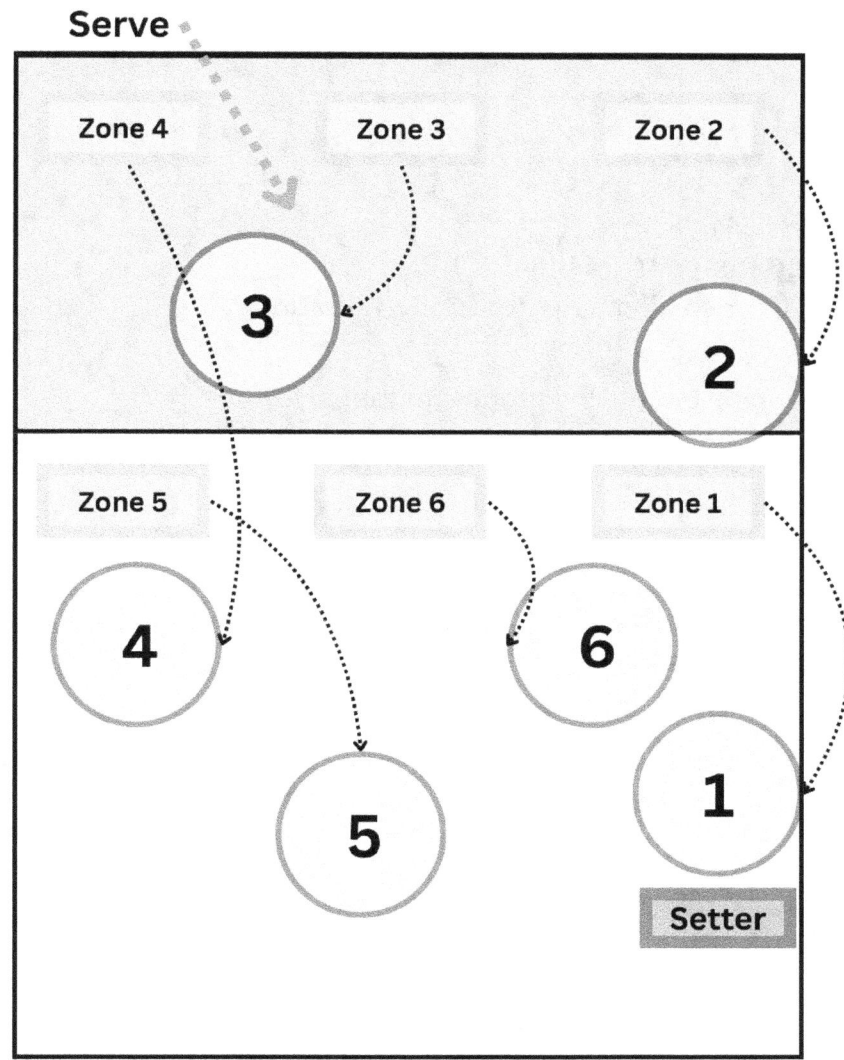

Figure 20. Score-pressure simulation displaying rotations and situational play under end-game conditions.

Primary Roles: All players.

Why This Matters

Matches are often decided not by talent but by composure. Pressure scenarios train athletes to execute fundamentals with focus when score, time, or fatigue raise the stakes.

What You'll Need

- Full court and scoreboard or timer.
- Two teams of 6 (or smaller sides for limited rotations).
- 8–10 volleyballs.
- Optional: whistle or buzzer for timed situations.

Let's Do It

1. Set a scenario (for example, 22-24, down two points, or 23-23 tie).
2. Play out rallies with the set conditions; the team must earn the final points to win.
3. Rotate serve and receive after each simulated set point.
4. Continue for 5 rounds, switching pressure situations (for example, match point, time limit, penalty serve).

Pro Tips from the Court

- Focus on breathing—steady inhale before each serve.
- Visualize success; confidence comes from rehearsal.
- Keep pre-point routines identical to reduce anxiety.

Take It Up a Notch

Add consequences to heighten focus—missed serve = push-ups, lost rally = sprint to baseline (30 ft / 9 m). Record win/loss ratio under pressure to measure composure improvement.

Common Mistakes & Fixes

- **Mistake:** Over-swinging under stress.
  - **Fix:** Simplify mechanics; rely on consistency.
- **Mistake:** Silence on the court.
  - **Fix:** Assign captains to lead communication cues.
- **Mistake:** Loss of tempo between points.
  - **Fix:** Reset the routine for every rally.

Benchmarks by Level

- **Beginner:** Wins 40% of pressure rounds.
- **Intermediate:** Wins 60% with controlled errors.
- **Advanced:** Wins 80% or more while maintaining full-speed execution.

How This Connects

Once players can handle scoreboard tension, they're ready for Drill 24 – Competitive Team Challenge, where every skill and mindset merges into full-game competition.

Coach's Note

Pressure is practice in disguise. If you can breathe here, you can breathe anywhere.

Drill 21: Advanced Read-Based Blocking

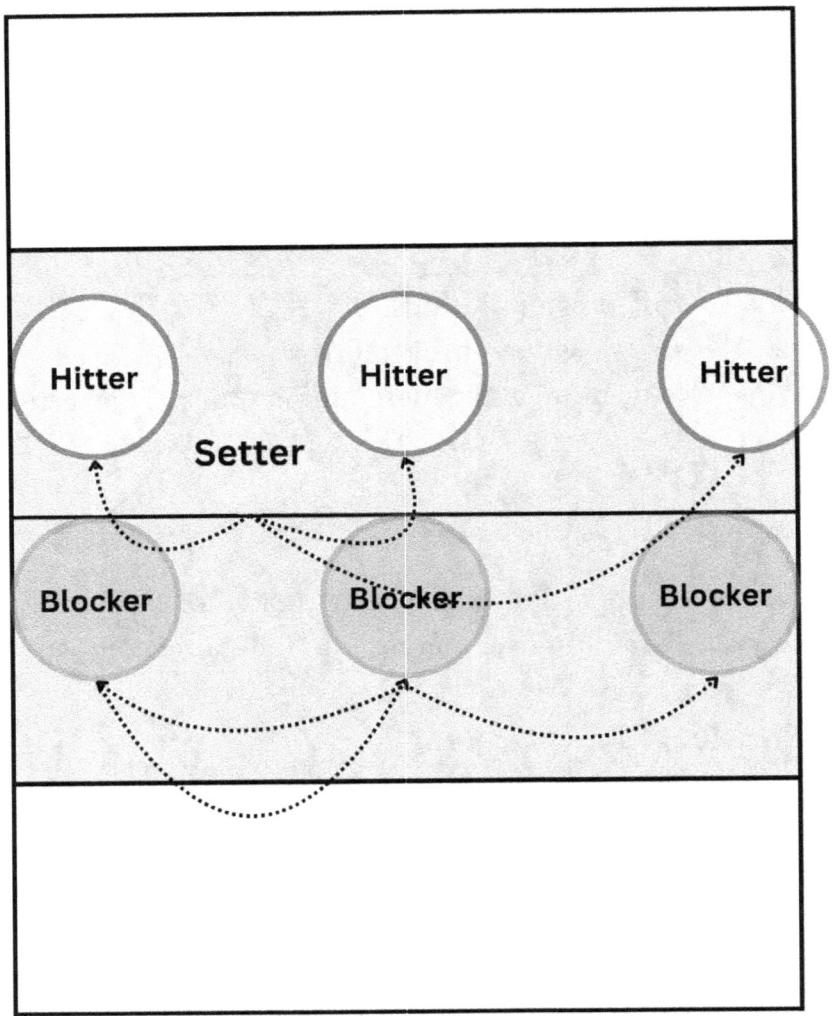

Figure 21. Read-based blocking keys showing setter cues and blocker movement paths.

Primary Roles: Middles, blockers, front-row hitters.

Why This Matters

Blocking isn't guessing—it's interpreting. This drill teaches players to read setter posture, hitter approach, and ball location to choose the correct block movement. It builds timing, coordination, and disciplined footwork across the front row.

What You'll Need

- Net and full front-row setup.
- 2–3 attackers.
- 1 setter.
- 8–10 volleyballs.
- Tape to mark block positions.

Let's Do It

1. The setter receives tossed balls and chooses one hitter (Zone 4, 3, or 2).
2. Blockers must:
    - Read the setter body line.
    - Identify the set location.
    - Execute proper footwork (shuffle or swing block).
3. The hitter attacks live while the blockers time and penetrate over the net.
4. Perform 10 reps, then rotate attackers.

Pro Tips from the Court

- Track the setter's shoulders—they point to where the set goes.
- Block hands should angle toward the attacker's chest, not straight up.
- Close the block seam with a quick final shuffle.
- Communicate "line," "angle," or "help" before the jump.

Take It Up a Notch

- Add fake sets or misdirection actions (for example, the setter jumps or raises hands as if setting one hitter, then delivers the ball to a different attacker).
- Introduce a back-row pipe attack to increase decision-making.
- Score performance: 1 point per well-timed block touch.

Common Mistakes & Fixes

- **Mistake:** Jumping straight up.
  - **Fix:** Focus on forward penetration.
- **Mistake:** Late read.
  - **Fix:** Watch the setter, not the ball.
- **Mistake:** Leaving seams open.
  - **Fix:** Keep hips connected with the partner blocker.

Benchmarks by Level

- **Beginner:** 5 well-timed blocks out of 10.
- **Intermediate:** 7 of 10 correct reads and penetrations.
- **Advanced:** 9 of 10 proper reads with successful block touches.

How This Connects

Effective blocking feeds directly into Drill 22 — Extended Rally Defensive Control, which builds the defensive stamina needed after blocked balls are kept in play.

Coach's Note

Great blockers defend before the ball crosses the net. Read first, jump second.

Drill 22: Extended Rally Defensive Control

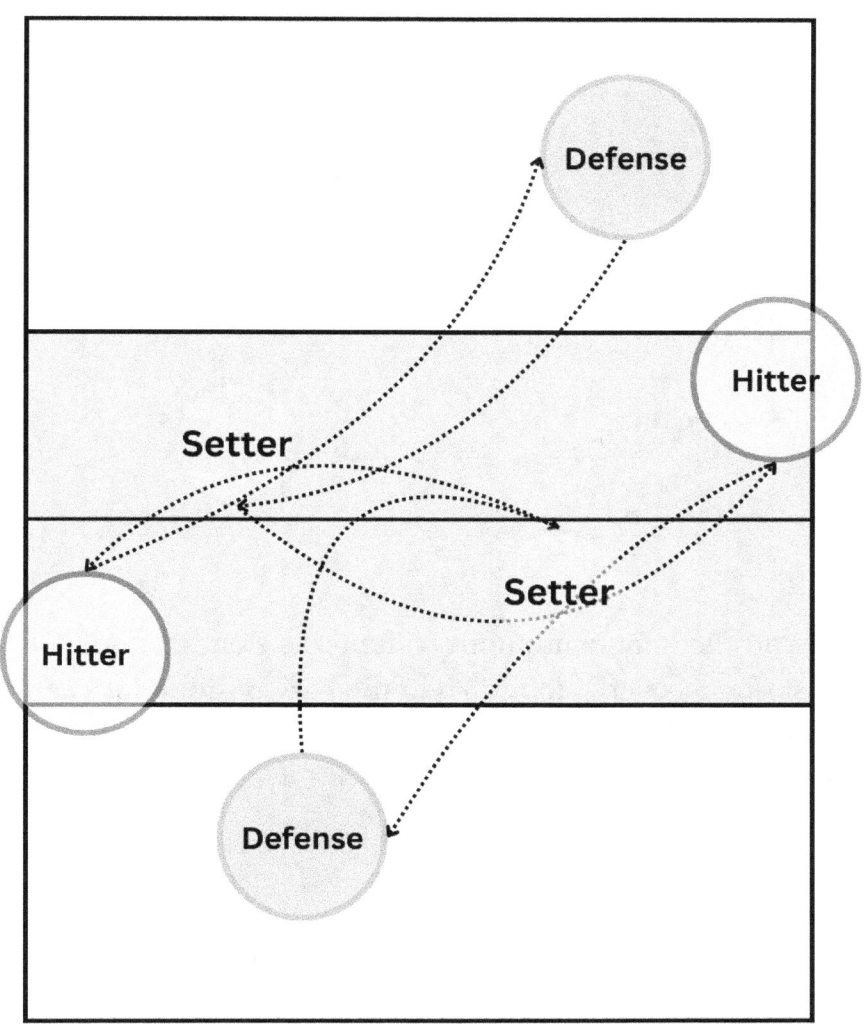

Figure 22. Extended rally defensive paths showing dig, reset, and coverage movement.

Primary Roles: Liberos, defensive specialists, all players.

Why This Matters

Long rallies test discipline, stamina, and mental control. This drill strengthens defensive recovery, positioning, and communication under 30–60 seconds of continuous, game-like pressure.

What You'll Need

- Half or full court.
- 3 attackers, 2 defenders, 1 setter.
- 10–12 balls.
- Timer set for 30–45 seconds.

Let's Do It

1. Attackers hit controlled but continuous balls across Zones 5 and 6.
2. Defenders must dig, recover, and return to the base position for each rep.
3. The setter sends the ball over or sets for controlled returns.
4. Continue nonstop for the designated time before switching roles.

Pro Tips from the Court

- Keep digs high (8–10 ft / 2.4–3 m) to allow resets.
- Stay low with forward momentum during movement.
- Breathe rhythmically—long rallies require composure.
- Use small shuffle steps, not long lunges.

Take It Up a Notch

- Increase rally duration to 60 seconds.

- Add random tip balls and roll shots.
- Introduce a third defender for rotational coverage.

Common Mistakes & Fixes

- **Mistake:** Fatigue leading to sloppy form.
    - **Fix:** Focus on breathing and footwork efficiency.
- **Mistake:** Collisions in deep court.
    - **Fix:** Assign clear lanes before each round.
- **Mistake:** Low digs.
    - **Fix:** Prioritize upward platform angle.

Benchmarks by Level

- **Beginner:** 10 clean digs per 30 seconds.
- **Intermediate:** 14–16 digs with controlled resets.
- **Advanced:** 18+ digs with strong transitions.

How This Connects

Extended rally discipline transitions smoothly to Drill 23 – Situational Serving Strategy, where decision-making under fatigue becomes tactical.

Coach's Note

Fatigue exposes flaws—disciplined defense fixes them.

Drill 23: Situational Serving Strategy

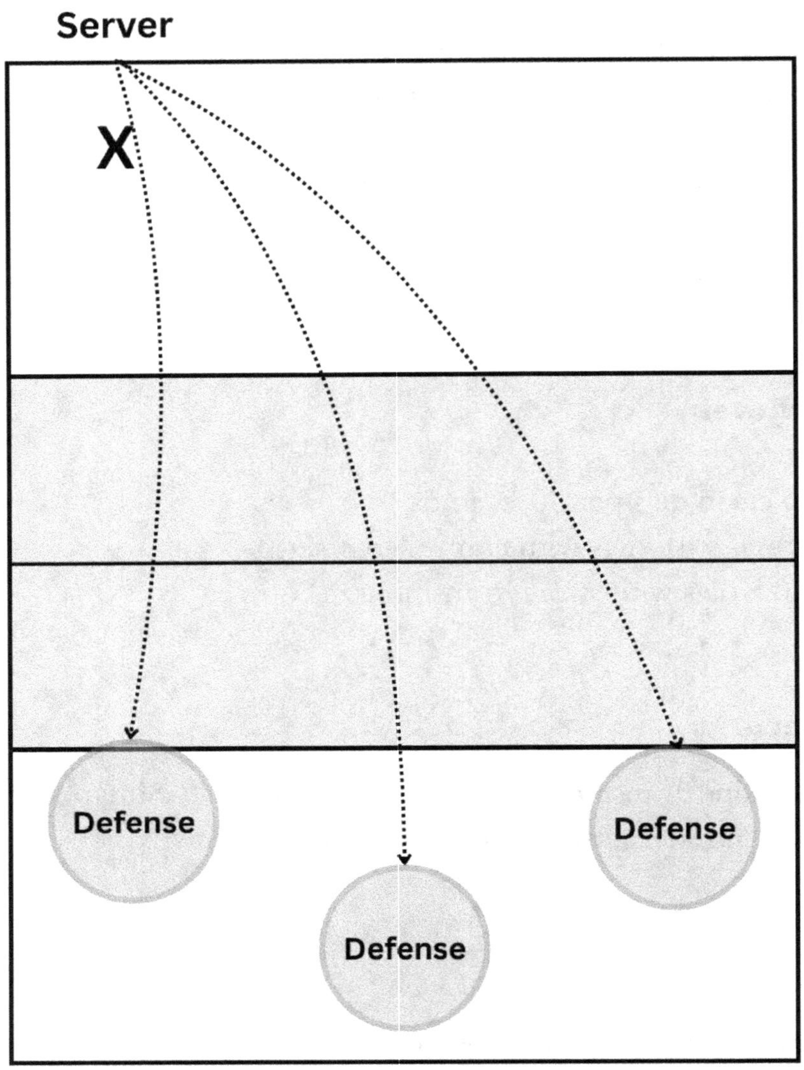

Figure 23. Situational serving zones illustrating tactical ball placement by scenario.

Primary Roles: Servers, all players.

Why This Matters

Serving isn't random—it's strategic. This drill teaches athletes to choose zones based on opponent weaknesses, rotation mismatches, and score scenarios. It builds volleyball IQ and targeted consistency.

What You'll Need

- Court with marked target zones.
- 1 server, 1–3 receivers.
- Rotation chart or scouting notes.
- 8–10 volleyballs.

Let's Do It

1. The coach assigns a scenario (for example, "serve Zone 1 to target the weak passer").
2. The server must hit the designated location with accuracy.
3. Continue through 6–8 scenarios, such as:
    - Avoid the star libero.
    - Serve short to disrupt a quick offense.
    - Deep to Zone 6 in high-pressure moments.
4. Track accuracy and decision-making.

Pro Tips from the Court

- Use calm, consistent toss mechanics.
- Visualize a zone before contact.
- Adjust power to avoid over-serving deep.
- Vary trajectories (float, hybrid, deep topspin).

Take It Up a Notch

- Add live passers who counter strategies.
- Combine two scenarios at once: "Zone 5 short AND avoid libero."
- Score accuracy: 1 point per successful tactical serve.

Common Mistakes & Fixes

- **Mistake:** Ignoring scouting cues.
    - **Fix:** Review target tendencies before serving.
- **Mistake:** Overthinking under pressure.
    - **Fix:** Keep the routine identical for each serve.
- **Mistake:** Serving too safely.
    - **Fix:** Aim confidently at edges.

Benchmarks by Level

- **Beginner:** 5 of 10 correct-zone serves.
- **Intermediate:** 7 of 10 with scenario alignment.
- **Advanced:** 9 of 10 with varied strategies.

How This Connects

Smart serving feeds directly into Drill 25 — Full-Court Chaos Game, where tactical decisions unfold in real time.

Coach's Note

Don't just serve the ball—serve the plan.

Drill 24: Competitive Team Challenge

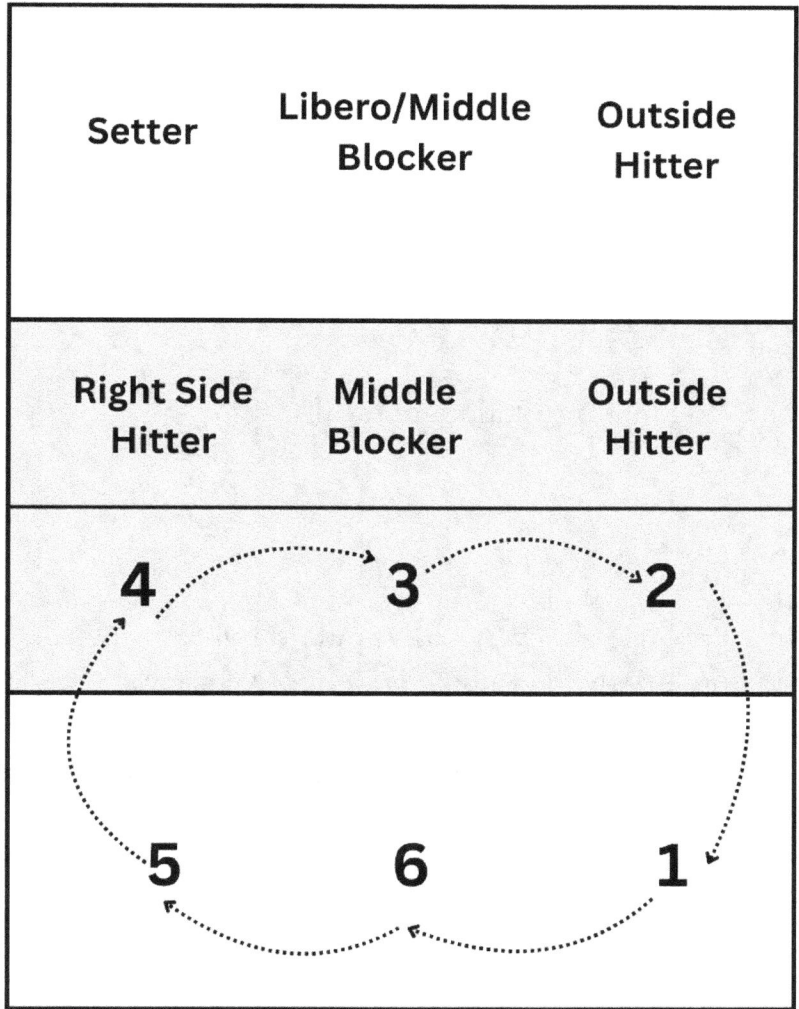

Figure 24. Full-team competitive challenge diagram showing six-player rotation and live match simulation.

Primary Roles: All players.

Why This Matters

Competition reveals mastery. This drill fuses every previous concept—technical skill, teamwork, and mental toughness—into a controlled scrimmage format that rewards consistency, communication, and grit.

What You'll Need

- Two full teams of 6 (or adjusted small-sided groups).
- Scoreboard or score-tracking sheet.
- 10+ volleyballs.
- A referee or coach to monitor rotations and calls.

Let's Do It

1. Play a match to 25 points (win by 2) with standard rally scoring.
2. Every 5 points, pause briefly to evaluate serve-receive accuracy, attack efficiency, and coverage success.
3. Coaches record stat targets: passing percentage, hitting percentage, serve accuracy, and total digs.
4. After one complete game, rotate lineups so all players experience each role.

Pro Tips from the Court

- Treat every rally as data—focus on process, not points.
- Use positive communication even during mistakes.
- Identify momentum swings and reset energy after each point.

Take It Up a Notch

Turn it into a mini-tournament. Keep cumulative stats across sessions and recognize "Top Server," "Best Passer," or "Most Composed Player." Track growth over weeks to visualize progress.

Common Mistakes & Fixes

- **Mistake:** Forgetting fundamentals in competitive mode.
  - **Fix:** Review key cues before each set.
- **Mistake:** Energy drop mid-game.
  - **Fix:** Rotate fresh servers or call timeout resets.
- **Mistake:** Players focus only on winning.
  - **Fix:** Set team goals around execution metrics, not points.

Benchmarks by Level

- **Beginner:** Complete one full game with consistent rotation and communication.
- **Intermediate:** Maintain 70% accuracy across serve, pass, and set stats.
- **Advanced:** Execute a full match series (best of 3) with recorded stat improvement week to week.

How This Connects

This final drill integrates everything from the program—serving precision, defensive reaction, offensive speed, and mental focus—into a complete match-ready performance routine.

Coach's Note

This is where work becomes play. Compete with pride, but never stop learning from each rally.

Drill 25: Full-Court Chaos Game

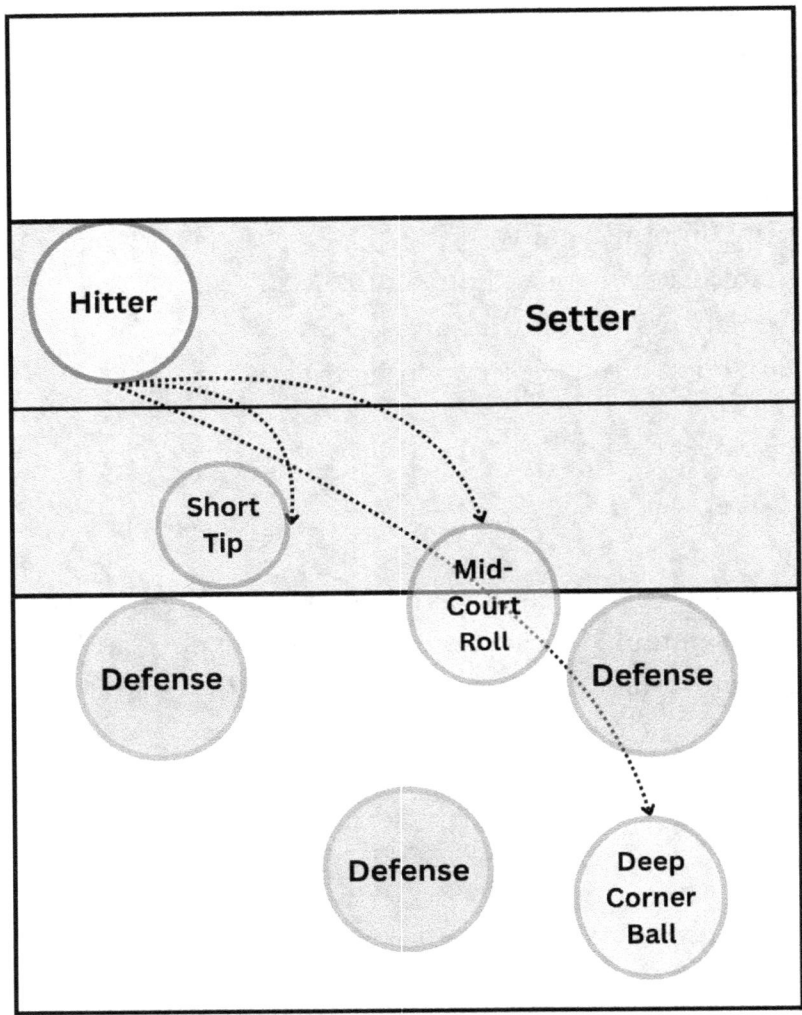

Figure 25. Full-court chaos rally illustrating random initiation and adaptive transitions.

Primary Roles: All players.

Why This Matters

Volleyball rarely unfolds in perfect patterns. Chaos training teaches adaptability—the ability to solve unpredictable, messy rallies with calm execution. This drill develops team decision-making under extreme variability.

What You'll Need

- Full court and 2 teams.
- Coach with a whistle.
- 10–12 volleyballs.
- Randomizer list (tips, rolls, out-of-system, back-row only, etc.)

Let's Do It

1. The coach initiates the rally with a random ball (short tip, deep corner, broken play, etc.).
2. Teams must adapt instantly, transitioning through dig → set → swing.
3. Every rally is different—the coach changes parameters each rep.
4. Play for 12–15 rallies, keeping score for execution (not just points).

Pro Tips from the Court

- Stay calm—chaos rewards patience.
- Use high-recovery balls to regain structure.
- Communicate roles quickly ("I'm up," "You take short").
- Maintain spacing even when the system breaks down.

Take It Up a Notch

- Add time pressure: must score within 2 swings.
- Limit certain skills (back row only, left side only).
- Introduce "bonus balls" worth 2 points.

Common Mistakes & Fixes

- **Mistake:** Freezing on unexpected plays.
  - **Fix:** Drill verbal cues ("tip," "deep," "reset").
- **Mistake:** Collapsing spacing.
  - **Fix:** Create lanes and hold them.
- **Mistake:** Panicked swings.
  - **Fix:** Encourage high balls to reset.

Benchmarks by Level

- **Beginner:** 6 functional rallies out of 12.
- **Intermediate:** 9 controlled rallies with resets.
- **Advanced:** 12+ chaos rallies with composure and execution.

How This Connects

This drill completes the entire training program. Chaos control ties together serving, passing, setting, blocking, coverage, and transition in one real-match experience.

Coach's Note

Anyone can look good in perfect conditions. Champions thrive in chaos.

Conclusion

Coaching volleyball is never just about the drills, the rotations, or the wins. It is about shaping experiences that help players grow as athletes and as people. Throughout this guide, you've explored the fundamentals of skill development, the structure of effective practices, the importance of team culture, and the tools to build resilience and mental toughness. Each section has been designed to give you practical steps you can apply immediately, while also encouraging you to think long-term—beyond a single season, toward building a sustainable program.

The role of a coach is both demanding and rewarding. It requires organization, patience, and clarity, as well as creativity, empathy, and adaptability. By combining technical knowledge with a player-first philosophy, you create an environment where athletes feel valued, supported, and challenged. That balance is what transforms a team from a group of individuals into a community that thrives together.

Remember that coaching is a journey. Every season brings new challenges, new lessons, and new opportunities to refine your approach. The drills and strategies in this book are tools, but the true impact comes from how you use them—with consistency, with care, and with a vision for growth.

As you move forward, keep the bigger picture in mind: the legacy of your coaching is not measured only in wins and losses, but in the confidence, resilience, and joy your players carry with them long after the final whistle. When you coach with purpose, you don't just build better athletes—you help shape stronger people.

Your journey as a coach continues. Lead with clarity, coach with heart, and trust that every practice, every game, and every moment matters.

References

American Volleyball Coaches Association (AVCA). *AVCA*. Accessed December 10, 2025. https://www.avca.org.

American Volleyball Coaches Association. *The Volleyball Coaching Bible*. Edited by Cecile Reynaud. Champaign, IL: Human Kinetics, 2015.

Fédération Internationale de Volleyball (FIVB). *FIVB*. Accessed December 10, 2025. https://www.fivb.com.

Hebert, Mike. *Thinking Volleyball*. Champaign, IL: Human Kinetics, 2014.

Human Kinetics. *Human Kinetics*. Accessed December 11, 2025. https://www.humankinetics.com.

Miller, Bob. *The Volleyball Handbook*. Champaign, IL: Human Kinetics, 2005.

National Collegiate Athletic Association (NCAA). *NCAA Women's Volleyball Resources*. Accessed December 10, 2025. https://www.ncaa.org.

USA Volleyball. *USA Volleyball*. Accessed December 9, 2025. https://www.usavolleyball.org.

Thanks for being a reader!

Thank you so much for being here. Writing this book wasn't just about teaching the basics—it was about reaching someone like you. Someone brave enough to start something new, to show up even when they're unsure, and to keep going even when it gets tough.

If this book helped you feel a little more confident, a little more seen, or a little more excited to play, then that means everything to me. I remember what it felt like to be new, to have questions, to feel lost on the court—and I wanted this to be the guide I wish I had back then.

If you got something out of these pages, I have one small favor to ask: would you consider leaving a quick review on Amazon? It doesn't have to be long. Just a few words about what helped you or what you liked.

Your review does more than you think—it helps other beginners find this book. People who might be nervous to start. People who just need a little encouragement to keep going. You can be that spark for someone else, just like this book might have been for you.

Just scan the QR code below. It only takes a minute, but it truly makes a big difference.

Thanks again for reading—and for being part of the volleyball community. Keep playing, keep growing, and never forget why you started.

– Riley Rush

www.ingramcontent.com/pod-product-compliance
Lightning Source LLC
Chambersburg PA
CBHW051352070526
44584CB00025B/3727